# Against the Forbidden Darkness:

A Medium and Her Struggle to Free Souls

A Novel Based on True Events

Anna Maria Manalo

2

Against The Forbidden Darkness: A Medium and Her Struggle to Free Souls.
Copyright (C) 2024 by Anna Maria Manalo

Published by The Sinister Archives Press.
All rights reserved.

No part of this book may be reproduced in any form or by any electronic or mechanical means, including information storage and retrieval systems, without written permission from the author except for the use of brief quotations in a book review.

For information, contact Cinescriber@gmail.com
www.annamariamanaloauthor.com

4

## Author's Note

This is a work of fiction based on the life of Michelle Budke, Founder of First City Paranormal of Kansas, Kansas, U.S. Names and locations of haunted homes, buildings and their owners have been changed when necessary in order to protect the individual or business. Any resemblance to actual places is purely coincidental.

6

## Other Books by Anna Maria Manalo

Nonfiction:

Portal: A Lifetime of Paranormal Experiences

The Way Through The Woods

Haunted Heirlooms

Unholy Structure

The Night Visitants

Fiction:

The Infernal

## Fiction Works in Progress:

The Shopkeeper of Salerno

The Isolationist

8

## Table of Contents

**Foreword by the Author**

**Part One:  Recognition**

Chapter One
Chapter Two
Chapter Three
Chapter Four
Chapter Five
Chapter Six
Chapter Seven
Chapter Eight
Chapter Nine
Chapter Ten
Chapter Eleven
Chapter Twelve
Chapter Thirteen
Chapter Fourteen
Chapter Fifteen
Chapter Sixteen
Chapter Seventeen
Chapter Eighteen
Chapter Nineteen
Chapter Twenty
Chapter Twenty One
Chapter Twenty Two

Chapter Twenty Three
Chapter Twenty Four
Chapter Twenty Five
Chapter Twenty Six
Chapter Twenty Seven
Chapter Twenty Eight
Chapter Twenty Nine
Chapter Thirty

## **Part Two:  Confrontation**

Chapter Thirty One
Chapter Thirty Two
Chapter Thirty Three
Chapter Thirty Four
Chapter Thirty Five
Chapter Thirty Six
Chapter Thirty Seven
Chapter Thirty Eight
Chapter Thirty Nine
Chapter Forty
Chapter Forty One
Chapter Forty Two
Chapter Forty Three
Chapter Forty Four

## **Part Three:  Attack**

Chapter Forty Five
Chapter Forty Six
Chapter Forty Seven
Chapter Forty Eight

Chapter Forty Nine
Chapter Fifty
Chapter Fifty One
Chapter Fifty Two
Chapter Fifty Three
Chapter Fifty Four
Chapter Fifty Five
Chapter Fifty Six
Chapter Fifty Seven
Chapter Fifty Eight
Chapter Fifty Nine
Chapter Sixty
Chapter Sixty One
Chapter Sixty Two
Chapter Sixty Three
Chapter Sixty Four
Chapter Sixty Five
Postscript

**Conclusion**

**First City Paranormal of Kansas Team Members in Alphabetical Order**

**Appendix: Prayers of Protection and Deliverance - Roman Catholic**

**About The Author**

12

For Rob Lemke

(1963 - 2021)

14

*"For we do not wrestle against flesh and blood, but against the rulers, against the authorities, against the cosmic powers over this present darkness, against the spiritual forces of evil in the heavenly places."*

*- Ephesians 6:12*

16

## Foreword from the Author

I met Michelle Budke online on a Facebook forum a few years ago while searching for a virtual assistant. I found the assistant, but also found Michelle: A faithful follower of my books who displayed a great fund of information in the realm of the supernatural. At that time I only had two books published by Beyond The Fray, a small and talented indie publisher who discovered me thru another publisher. It just went from there to where I am now.

For an author like me who earnestly began writing upon early retirement in the spring of 2020, Michelle came at the perfect time in my new career as a creative nonfiction author and novelist. Disenchanted with the ongoing politics of my job as a school counselor, marginalized as an Asian woman of high caliber, Michelle and the collective embrace of the paranormal community was a welcome respite. The supernatural intrigued me from the beginning of my childhood, peppered my life with both tragedy, shock and amazement, and her arrival at a forefront of a second career for me was a gift.

I was surprised by Michelle's earnest manner and simplicity despite her innate giftedness with all things unseen. As I struggled with polishing my art and craft as a previous screenwriter, Michelle's presence online punctuated my works and efforts with continued support. I began in earnest to reach out, piqued by her loyal interest and the correspondence blossomed in what would become a close collaboration of spiritual interests.

In time, Michelle's revelations fueled and compelled me to learn more about this highly complex woman who exuded an energy and a knowledge that transcended her simple life and background. As the new year unfolded, Michelle finally penned a chronology of events of her life for me to read. What I read of her world pushed the limits of my three-dimensional thinking - and my desire to scribe her narrative inspired by events in her life bordered on obsession.

I present to you the volume inspired by Michelle's story.

Anna Maria Manalo
April 18, 2024
Petit - Bersac, Dordogne, France

19

**Part One:**

**Recognition**

# Chapter One

## Post-Pandemic

The wind whips through Michelle's jacket as she emerges from the house onto the grass, her blonde hair obscuring her eyes. She pins her hair back with both hands and turns to survey the old brick home, the grime and molded shutters betraying years of neglect and abandonment. A year after the pandemic, the tenants had fled after their forced confinement in the old house. An old house with a history punctuated by slaves left to neglect and abandoned after a fallow harvest. Trees surrounded the house and swayed as if to warn her, but Michelle stood firmly rooted to the ground and entranced despite the ominous weather. It had taken a sudden turn since they entered an hour ago. She listens for something, almost trancelike and akin to a Buddhist monk in meditation.

The light of late afternoon was fading into night and an impenetrable gloom descended on the desolate house. She waits as she ties her thick hair back, eyes focused on the dark but open front door as the trees trilled their song. Everything creaked, including the door, as if threatening to shut in the rest of the crew. Leaves fragile and spent disengage themselves from limbs, littering the grass wet with a translucent sheen and some alighted near Michelle as if to inspect her.

A young woman in her early thirties emerges, Michelle's daughter, Jessica. She joins her mother, her sneakers scrunching underfoot, breaking Michelle's reverie. A scent assails Michelle from the open front door: Loneliness, decay and a tinge of sadness as if the house was screaming for company in its solitude.

It was.

23

A third woman emerges. Unlike Jessica, Nancy was older, but her charming smile and disarming warmth radiated youth. Michelle approaches the woman who is a good friend. She gives the woman's hand a reassuring squeeze. Michelle found herself sensing a gnawing disquiet within. Then a fourth, a young man in his twenties exits the door. Jake's features betray that he is surely Jessica's brother, Michelle's younger child. An only son. Blonde too, he is sure-footed, confident and towers over the three women. Unlike Jessica and Nancy, he exuded an air of detachment. Unflappable like his mother, he eyes the house and the surrounding wood with an air akin to an inspector checking an old house. He carries a large duffel with him which he places on the ground before pulling the front door shut with a reassuring tug. He grabs the duffel and turns to join the group.

Jake spots his mother listening for something only she can hear and breaks her reverie. "When are the owners returning?"
"They're not."
"They're not?"
"No."
"I can't say I blame them. Too much tragedy in a home."
"It would be for me, anyway." Adds Nancy. "Especially being confined to a place like that."
"It would be for me too." Michelle pauses and then leads the group to the car, a Jeep Cherokee in white. "I meant, it's too much, but I must come back to cleanse it."
"For who, Mom? Jessica asks. "They abandoned it… and left it in disrepair."

Michelle enters the driver's side and pauses to watch her daughter pull the seatbelt around her chest on the passenger seat. She adjusts the rearview mirror in time to see Nancy and Jake fasten their belts with a snap. They appeared somber and reticent as they looked up expectantly.
"For them it's just a home, but I have to release whosoever is left in the house." She ends.
"I have to give the ghosts closure… then it will be bought… and fixed."

24

The silence in the car takes hold as Michelle ponders how much she sensed and saw.

"There's people there, maybe even a child. I hear them. They're begging for help." She adds.

Nancy's breath catches in reply. Michelle looks up her rearview mirror. "I have to send them to the light."

"Is that what you mean, Mom?" Jake ventures.

"Yes. I can't let someone else occupy this house while there's spirits living there. Sometimes the present and the past can't live together."

"I wonder if people would feel what you feel in this place." Nancy adds. "She can." Jessica replies as she pointedly glances at her mom, her blue eyes shining with support.

"How do you know, Mom?" Jake adds. "The equipment only went off once... I mean the EVP. Could be artifact."

"There was more."

"Old houses put out an aura..." Jake rebuts.

"I meant, it's more than that. Some the EVP and even the cameras don't get."

"You're alone in that." Jake adds. Michelle nods. "I am, it seems. But your uncles would've sensed it too. Uncle Rob for sure."

"I miss Uncle Rob."

"I do too." Michelle's voice begins to break.

"I did feel the creepiness... especially the stairs... that area." Nancy volunteers. It confirmed for Michelle how she sensed the woman's internal anxiety.

Michelle nods. "Being watched?" Nancy nods from the back seat.

"You're coming back? With us, I hope?" Jessica asks with trepidation.

"I have to. If I can, with you all."

"When Mom?" Jessica and Jake both said in unison.

"It would have to be soon and with Jane along."

"Jane will help us if there's a curse too. Her drums." Adds Nancy.

Michelle cringes as she steps on the gas and slides the vehicle onto the narrow road, lined with fields on either side in the darkness.

25

"You okay, Mom?" Jessica peers at the face of her mother.

"Yes." Michelle lies. Pain shoots from her lower abdomen to her solar plexus and onto her neck like a viselike grip.

"Mom. I can drive." Jessica touches her mother's hand.

"No. I meant I'm fine. Just getting used to the back brace being off."

Michelle hears Nancy's concerned intake of breath. Her eyes instinctively pop to the rearview mirror. "How's your back healing?"

Behind the SUV, the driveway she just left glistens with dew.

Michelle steers the wheel, exiting onto the pavement. "It's healing, but slowly. I just have to be careful nothing attaches itself to our equipment."

"Or to you." Jessica adds.

A few feet behind the car, a figure stands watching in the center of the driveway, his arms clasped behind him. Even in the gloaming, he appeared weather-beaten, gaunt and bespoke of an earlier era. In the half-light, his exhaustion and desperation was evident, his cheeks sunken, his eyes pleading.

In her head, Michelle heard "Come back."

She telegraphs her thoughts: "I promise." Then, she chants the Our Father and the rest join in unison as the car disappears into the night.

The back door blasts open and slams onto the wall to betray the darkness of the street. October had taken its usual turn as halloween approached. Outside, a plastic skeleton sways, hung on the back porch of a stuccoed house across the street as if signaling the season as it danced in reply. Somewhere nearby, wind chimes sung the sound of protest.

The tinkling of the chimes reminds David, a man in his late fifties, of spring. He hurriedly shuts the refrigerator in the yellow and white kitchen, dark with only the

26

nightlight. The refrigerator clicks, shifting the light to darkness as he rushes to the back door. He pushes it against the night, turning the one bolt home. Silence.

It seems to David that since his wife's team visited the haunted home a few nights ago, the weather had taken a sudden turn for the worse. He pulls his robe around him, fastening it as he shivers and makes his way back to a glass of milk on the counter. His thoughts turn to his wife who the previous evening courageously returned to the house to 'release' the spirit and send it to the light. It was, according to Michelle, a house where slaves had died destitute under the hands of a plantation owner who left them to starve.

Michelle's demeanor was one of unbridled joy when she returned earlier that night. He was so glad she was safe and unharmed by the house of restless souls. In a gesture of love, he massaged her feet and made Chamomile tea for her despite the exhaustion in his eyes from worry. He knew she was still recovering from back surgery, the aches and pains issuing like a knife that traveled down her back, now healing and manageable. Then, world-weary, she trudged up the stairs to their bedroom.

David sips, then his face turns sour. He pours it down the sink. On the way out of the kitchen, he spies a tin and opens it. Oatmeal cookies. David reaches in like a child, bites through, but he suddenly pulls his foot away in fright. The long haired brown and white cat was brushing against his leg, her eyes luminous and flecked with worry like his. David sighs in relief. He had been jittery lately.

"Kelly. What's the matter, baby girl?"
He chews and picks up the cat with one arm as he saunters up the steps back to the bedroom. In the deep recesses of his mind, David wonders whether he was projecting his own worries on the cat. She purred as he carried her towards the bedroom, but then he notes her hairs stand on end.

27

He pauses. He thought he heard wings flapping behind the closed door. Large wings like that of an albatross. Perhaps more like an eagle, David ponders, as he is in Kansas. Suddenly the cat leaps and darts back down the stairs.
Behind him, another bedroom door opens down the hall. Jake, a study in pajamas stare back, sleep still in his eyes.
"Did you hear that, Dad?" He whispers.

Wings flap, then an impenetrable silence. A female moan.
"It's Mom." Jake offers and darts for the master bedroom past his father.
Dave turns the knob to their room as Jake joins him.

In the half-light of the sheer curtains, David sees something clutching the edge of the wooden floorboard of the large bed. It intently stares down at Michelle who lay uneasily turning under the sheets as if in the throes of a nightmare, her eyes shut as she continued an internal struggle. She moaned. David approached and the creature turned to eye him. It had the visage of a human, but with the outline of a bat. David's head screamed in terror, but his lips failed. A palpable sense of menace and hate assailed them.

David finally let out a gasp as Jake held up a stick of sorts.

The creature eyes Jake and unfolded its wings in reply. Dave backed away, stunned at its sheer size.

"Get out!" Jake yelled as he approached, both hands in a viselike grip around a metal stick. David stared in shock at his son and realized he was holding his prized golf putter. Slowly, he looked back to where his son focused his eyes and discovers a growling visage of hate.

The creature opened its mouth, eyes red. Then it turned and flew through the closed glass of the window.
The men stood speechless and then bolted down the stairs in pursuit.

28

Michelle sat up from the bed. Too fast. She saw stars as her heart pounded. Her back shot in a paroxysm of pain, reminding her of the stitches that still pulled when she made a sudden move.
Footsteps. Yelling. She heard her husband's voice and then her son's, as the front door sprung open below. She senses malice in the aftermath, a cloying scent of animal dung and a fear grips her as she reaches for the edge of the bed.

Michelle gingerly steps onto the carpeted floor and approaches the window, pulling it up. She grimaced with effort.

Her husband and son were on the front walk, surveying the road and the surrounding neighborhood. Searching, it seemed. David looked up and they locked eyes.

"Come back. Please." Michelle yells from the window. She turns and feels something stare her down, but there was nothing there. Michelle knew it was gone, but out of habit, she approaches the closet. Opening the closet door, she inspects the clothes in their hangers. She moves each one methodically and then looks up at the shoeboxes.

She takes one box out and opens it. A metal cross. A vial of holy water labeled "Medjugorje." She takes it out and begins to intone a prayer, closing her eyes. A hand touches and stays, the warmth penetrating her shoulder. It was David.

"You're okay?" He asked with uncertainty. Behind him stood Jake, eyes wary, still holding the putter. "Mom, didn't you see something like that when you were a teenager?"

"Yes, like a Mothman. Glad you woke me. It was, I thought, in my dreams."
"Is it back?"
"I hope not."

29

"I'll keep the lights on and stay up a bit until you sleep, honey." David offered.
Jake makes for the hallway, retiring for the night. "Yell if you need me, Dad."
"I think it's gone… for now. Go to bed, son. Glad you're staying with us."
"Okay, Mom?"
"Thank you. I am." Michelle replies. She turns and looks at the closet and is lost
in a distant memory. The closet is deep and dark as Michelle ponders and recalls a
childhood room.

30

## Chapter Two

## 1973

The closet is as deep as it was dark, like a night riven with phantoms. Charlene, a young woman in her late twenties with blonde hair and brilliant blue eyes studies it, her lips pursed as she puzzles. Her eyes, a study flecked in blues and greens dart like a firefly as her body tenses to explore the small room inside her daughter's boudoir. She pins her thick hair back into a pony tail and finally enters the walk-in closet, a rarity in the cul-de-sac of the neighborhood of their new home.

Charlene surveys her baby daughter's frilly dresses hanging from little pink and yellow hangers. She leans closer, touching one little dress and inhales the fresh and characteristic scent of a five year old child: Fresh, lightly scented and reminiscent of cotton candy. However, there was something else that yielded to her senses that brought with it an inescapable sense of comfort. She lovingly touches the clothes one by one, as if to count them. The familiarity of the clothing and the unique scent that accompanied her daughter appeared to be reassuring her despite the strangeness of her surroundings and what had just happened the night before. Charlene heard herself exhale in relief.

On three shelves under the small clothes, little pairs of pants, shorts and other blouses and tee shirts were neatly folded and stacked according to kind. Charlene herself had done them a few days ago when she had finally unpacked the laundry detergent and bleach, placing them in the new laundry area in the basement of the new house. She found herself instinctively setting up not just the laundry room but the children's closets. Methodically, like the energizer bunny from the battery ad,

32

she made her way towards the front of the hallway by the stairs: To the master bedroom.

As Charlene paced with restless energy, she found what she had earlier thought she had misplaced during the relentless unpacking of boxes to make the new house a home: A large rose-colored box laden with felt on top of the bureau near her husband's folded ties. Inside the box, two expensive-looking scissors, an electric razor and fine combs in differing sizes sat in a row like silent soldiers. Charlene made a mental note to place it in the car with her when she returned to work the following week. The trappings of her trade.

In the master bath closet, Charlene observes where she had stashed the remaining bed clothes after making the beds, where she recalled covering each child's bed, each one, with a blanket against the night chill. She distinctly remembered her hands doing each chore from basement to the upstairs rooms and folding the bed clothes after the salon sprays and scissors were checked and rechecked. She glanced around, vexed that she could somehow forget to provide blankets to shelter the children from the unpredictably stiff breezes of the Kansas night.

How could she? They could have easily caught a cold.

Charlene prided herself in her precision, sense of patterns and cleanliness, the home where she excelled in all things sewing, embroidery and the antiques she found herself collecting. She even unpacked with great care her tea set, her porcelain dolls and figurines. She made sure her special scissors were sharp and disinfected with hot water and soap and placed in an alcohol bath to keep it antiseptic. But somehow she failed last night with the children. She chose not to bring it up with Larry as he approached the dinner table exhausted from work. A fluke. It wouldn't happen again.

As Charlene checks the minutia of Michelle's closet, still perturbed, she finally reaches to close both doors of the closet. She turns and darts from the little bedroom with its pink-laced four poster and exits into the hallway. Outside, she absently rubs her chin and strolls to her sons' bedroom at the end of the hall, in the process passing a window with a deep recess where she had placed cushions. She fluffs the cushions, all new in a medley of blues and greens.

She pauses in shock.

That's when she spots it. Michelle's blanket. Then, under the daughter's were Ron's and Rob's. All three children's blankets, neatly folded and stacked on the hallway window seat. Charlene does a double take, appalled. She scratches her head in consternation and then sighs. She reaches for them and darts to her sons' bedroom.

Charlene makes a mental note to remember how she unfolded Ron's bed down with the blanket of navy blue and purple ships. Again. Then, she follows the same procedure with Rob's, folding the sheet over the blanket, smoothing it over. Again. This blanket was a purple and green quilt her mother had made. Finally, now exhausted from her chores, Charlene wearily returns to her only daughter's bedroom across from the master bedroom. The youngest and only girl had the largest room with the walk-in closet she had examined earlier. She re-enters and senses something off, but she couldn't put her finger on it.

Charlene ignores her internal compass, tossing it up to the strangeness of a new house. She positions the blanket as she did with the boys, folding the sheet over and then making a fold where her little girl would enter the bed. She backs away, satisfied and smooths the bedding's surface.

Below, she hears the doorbell ring not once, but several times. A sense of urgency.

Ron stood at the threshold, his beige shorts riddled with grass stains. His eight-year-old face registered a look of consternation as Charlene beheld her son. "Mom, quick!"

34

Ron dashes down the porch and runs to the edge of the house to the neighboring yard.

"What is going on?" Charlene hurriedly darts after her son.

A cluster of neighborhood children stood in a circle around a boy lying on the grass. They stood by a willowy tree at the edge of the property, looking down. Ron reenters the circle of children and Charlene notes her daughter in shorts waving frantically to Rob as another woman approaches from the house on their left. Rob, Charlene's oldest at ten, knelt on one leg as he inspects the child on the grass who appeared about Ron's age.

The children part as Charlene approaches. She recognized the boy with brownish hair who lived next door. He lay face up, staring at the sky with a sickly grin on his face. He appeared to be snickering. Above his head were what appeared to be animal bones and skulls, hanging from strings like a Christmas tree gone dark and foul.

"What happened?" Charlene gawks at the skulls, cupping her mouth in a gesture of disgust.

"He kinda just went goofy on us." Rob replied, standing up and brushing the grass off his knees, evading the bones over his head.

"My Tim! Tim! Did he fall from the tree?" This came from the other woman who walked over from the adjacent house. Charlene reaches for the boy's hand. "Are you able to get up?"

"Mom, don't touch him!" Rob exclaims, backing away.

"Why?"

"A little man went to him." Charlene turns to discover her daughter standing next to her.

"Yeah. Must be." Rob agrees with his little sister. The other children nod in unison and begin to back away, now afraid.

"Tell me what happened to my son!" The woman exclaims, cradling the boy on the ground. "Someone call an ambulance!"

35

Suddenly, the boy sits up on his own and begins to laugh. "I was real dizzy from the tree, Mommy."

"A tree made you dizzy?" The woman asked as she reached for her son, touching his forehead as if to check for a temperature. She pulls him up and away from the tree. "Maybe a bee stung you?"

"I'm fine, mom!" Tim swats his mother's hands away.

"I told you! It's from THAT tree." Another boy states, pointing at the willow tree. "Now tell us what's really going on here!" Charlene sternly queries.

"Mom, we dared him." Rob finishes.

"I'm sorry. Do you need help?" Charlene offers to the woman who now takes the boy by the hand, slapping him on the thigh.

"No, he's just being his usual prankster self. Come on home. How can a tree make you dizzy, you brat? You scared the life out of me."

"What are those dead skulls, Mom?" Ron ventures. Charlene grabs Michelle and ushers the two boys away towards their home.


Charlene sat on the kitchen table, the formica's surface newly scrubbed. Both boys and Michelle sat across from her. The evening shadows takes a hold of the kitchen and the lights began to glow.

"I want the truth."

"Mom, Michelle told you. We were just playing and everyone dared Tim to sit under the tree…"

"Why? What's in the tree?"

"You know…". Ron and Rob eye each other and become silent.

Charlene looked from one child to the other.

"I don't know. That's why I'm asking you both. Who put those skulls there?" Charlene sighs as she glances at the clock. It was almost time to make dinner. Both boys shrugged with a look.

"Mommy?" Michelle speaks up.

"Yes, hon?"

"That tree had a short man living in it."

36

"I see. You saw?" Charlene nods knowingly as if speaking a nursery rhyme.
"No Mom, she's right. She's telling you... it had a hat on..." Rob states
defensively.
"Mommy? It sat like this..." Michelle's diminutive voice plaintively states as she
mimes someone in the act of sitting. She ends up flopping onto the tile floor.
Michelle giggles, covering her mouth.
"Sat on what, honey?"
"The short man in the tree came out... like this... And then.. and then..."
"...and then, Michelle?" Charlene prods.
"The man made him dizzy and strange."
"Has anyone seen this man before?"
"Nope." Ron offers.
"Oh, yeah." Rob pipes up, as his eyes glow as if recalling an incident.
"Go. Tell me." Charlene prods.
"He lives in the tree." Michelle ends as she points to the backyard past the large
kitchen window.
"He's like a neighbor." Rob adds.

Charlene walked over to the kitchen window and looks out. Just a few yards
ahead, the backyard lay now in a long lazy shadow of late afternoon. Past the tree
near the border of the neighbor's property, the larger tree stood with the skulls
dangling. Charlene points, asking the two boys.
"You keep your sister away from that tree from now on, you hear?"

37

## Chapter Three

Michelle dozes on her side under the soft blanket, facing the window. Behind her, the door to the bedroom stood ajar, a soft nightlight casting a faint blue glow from the hallway. Several feet past her feet, the walk-in closet began to emit a light from within, emitting under the door and over it. The two doors began to slowly swivel open, allowing a reddish glow to enter the child's bedroom.

A shapeless mass like black ink, pools from the closet floor towards the four-poster bed. It appears to slither, then pool, slither, then pool. It pauses as if to take in its surroundings.
Then it slithers forward again.

Above the four-poster, where the lace from the headboard formed a heart, the face of an embroidered cherubim graced the four-poster over the sleeping child. Michelle slept under the protective glance of the angel, unaware of the resonant hum that steadily grew.

Suddenly, the pool of darkness stopped slithering. The hum stops.

The figure of a young girl stood a few yards away from Michelle's bed, her features obscured as she stood with her face in shadow, the window behind her. In the dim light, she wore white shoes with lace stockings and a blue dress with a white pinafore. The street light from the window behind her cast a glow on her figure, marking the outline of her dress and giving it an ethereal glow. Her face comes to view as she approaches Michelle's bed, glancing down to touch the bedding and to study the visage of the sleeping child. She could be an older sister of ten, the resemblance striking, save for the dark hair.

A breeze blew. The light from the child disappeared and with it, the child.

39

Then, Michelle yawned and turned to face the bedroom door.

She slept.

Down the hall, Rob and Ron's room lay at the end of the hall. Rob, a light sleeper, mumbles as his eyes fluttered with a movement he detected barely from wakefulness. Too sleepy, he submitted to a hum that placed him in a deeper slumber.

Nearby, Ron moved a foot under the bedclothes, deep inside his sleep, the onset of a dream, perhaps. The blue blanket, a calico pattern sewn by Charlene, moved. Something slowly pulls it off his arm, down to his stomach, exposing his small thin body in his beige pajamas adorned with sailboats. He does not notice.

The blanket, pulled by an unseen hand continues down to his legs and finally drops in a flat pile off the bed and onto the cold wooden floor. Nearby, Rob continues to mumble in his sleep as his blanket sails off his body, exposing his own pajamas. This too settles on the floor, but now both blankets are moving towards the bedroom door.

The night light glows and then fizzles. Rob shivers in his sleep, unable to awaken. Ron lies still as a breeze enters through the closed window. The streetlight flickers outside the window. The hum intensifies.

Charlene's eyes flick open. Something is off. Definitely off. She sits up, an internal alarm in the back of her heart tells her she must get up. She studies the prone form of her husband, who lay on his back. His snore was soft, his breathing regular. Satisfied it wasn't him that awakened her, Charlene surveys the dim room and slowly and with stealth swings her feet, grabbing the rose-colored robe from the edge of the bed. She didn't want to awaken her tired husband who needed his sleep unless necessary. Charlene listens as she pushes her small feet into the warmth of her Dearfoam slippers.

Call it the instinct of a mother, Charlene softly pads across the floor and peers through the bedroom door, slightly ajar. She listens. A memory of her own peaceful childhood tinges her face. The evenness of night in a new home when she was a child, her own parents reading to her by the lamp and then tucking her in with a prayer. She hears the sounds of the night from her position and it drifts her into a memory of the street in her childhood home. She sees the flicker of the streetlamp, pulling her into the present from her memory. She emerges into the hall to look out the deep window lined with pillows. No blankets were folded on the deep seat of the window sill this time. She sighs and returns to the bedroom.

The clock showed almost three a.m. How long had she been standing there, daydreaming?

Charlene approaches the bed and then hears the floorboards creak. She decides to check on the children. Outside in the hallway, Charlene glances at her daughter's bedroom door, slightly ajar and across from their own bedroom. She silently pushes the door open and enters.

Michelle's sleeping form lay still and a soft breeze issues from the window. Charlene approaches the window and rechecks to make sure it was shut. She turns, her daughter's back to her. She approaches the still figure, lovingly pulling the sheet up to cover Michelle's back.

Then, in surprise, Charlene backs up. She searches the bed. The blanket is gone again, leaving the sheet behind. She touches Michelle's nightgown and feels the chill on her daughter's bare arm. She surveys the room, now taken aback as she searches for the blanket again. She approaches the closet, slowly opening both sides of the door. The hinges creak.

With trepidation, Charlene looks in and hears a distinct hum issuing from somewhere in the room. She pulls away and shuts it. She surveys the shelves of toys, the clowns and dolls staring back at her as if hovering over a question. Where is it? Where is Michelle's blanket?

Charlene darts to the door, exits the hallway and makes for her sons' bedroom.

Both boys lay asleep. Rob lay with one leg dangling over the bed as if drunk, no blanket. His mouth was half-open. Ron lay on his side, the sheet askew on his form. Their still form lay with just the thin cover of the sheets she had placed there before covering the bedding with a blanket. She surveyed the room, knowing now she wouldn't find either blanket. Mesmerized by the unexplainable events, she stood frozen. A wisp of air hits her and she turns to the bedroom door. She hastily exits.

Into the living room, then the family room, Charlene darts, examining the sofas and the chairs for signs of the blankets. Baffled, she enters the kitchen and sees the gleaming counter devoid of last night's dinner, clean, empty except for the teapot on a doily. She sighs and wraps her robe tightly around her.

Charlene descends the stairs to the basement.

Halfway down, she detects a pile at the bottom step. She turns on the light. There, on the bottom step, neatly folded, were the three blankets.

43

## **<u>Chapter Four</u>**

"You took my blankeeet?"

"No."

"Are you sure?"

"Yes."

"Mommy told Daddy it disappeared."

"What do you think happened?"

"Rob and Ron lost their blankeeets too."

"I know."

"You know?"

"Yes."

"How?"

"I see things."

"You do?"

"You see things too."

"I do?"

The girl nodded, her blue dress shimmering in the light from the window.

"You know a lot."

"You do too, Michelle." The girl smiles.

"Who do you think took our blankeeets?"

"Cold people."

"Cold people?"

The girl nodded solemnly. She points at the walk-in closet.

Michelle turns from the edge of the bed where she sat. "There?"

"Yes."

"Like the vampire neighbors?"

"Sort of. But we shouldn't talk about them."

"Why?"

"Because they may be listening."

44

Michelle looks on, eyes wide at the closet. "They live there?"
A creak issues from the closet. Michelle leaps into the bed, pulling the blankets over her shoulders and stares at the girl. "Did you hear that?"
"Yes."
"Stay here with me, Mary Michelle."
"Go." The girl points to the door as her eyes widen at something on the floor.
"Where?"
"Go, Michelle. Now." The girl points towards the bedroom door.
"Go to Mommy?"
"Yes. Go to Mommy and Daddy."
"Come with me, Mary Michelle."
"Don't be afraid. I will watch you go."

Michelle leaps from the bed and dashes out of the room. The girl watches.

Charlene softly pads towards the bed and pauses. Nature called and she made a turn towards the en suite bathroom. Inside, she hears small feet slip down the hallway and a whooshing sound proclaims their bedroom door had opened. Quickly, Charlene wipes herself, now wondering what would awaken her next. The blankets troubled her the night before, steadily inching into her awareness and Larry's that the house may be haunted. She felt a sense of unease as he wondered if tonight would reveal the blankets taken again or perhaps a specter now ready to accost her outside the bathroom.

Gingerly, Charlene turns the knob and exits back into the stillness of the dark room. The figure of a child in a pink nightgown stood in the moonlight. She gasps.

"Mommee?"
Charlenes lets out a sigh of relief. "Yes, Michelle?"
Charlene watches her baby girl of five softly pad towards her as she leans down to pick her up.

45

"I want to stay here." Michelle states, one finger in her mouth.

Larry stirs in his sleep. "Come." He gestures to Michelle.

Charlene watches her daughter happily dart to the bed, grateful of the welcome. She lies on her side, curled up facing her father as Charlene joins them, pulling the blankets up to her neck.

"You had a nightmare, sweetie?"

"I don't think so."

"What is it then?" Larry ventures, facing the child.

"There's people in the closet."

"Oh." Charlene exclaims as Larry winks at her in the dark.

"How? Did you see them?" Larry ventures.

"No, Daddy."

"Well, then how do you know…". Charlene prods, playing with the gold locks of her daughter's hair. It was the same color as hers.

"They might have taken the blankeeets last night."

Charlene gasped. She had not told her that her blanket and brothers' blankets had disappeared the night before and that she put them back on after finding them in a pile in the basement.

Larry looks back at Charlene pointedly eyeing her as if to say, no, I didn't tell her.

"Who told you they might have, honey?"

Michelle paused, sucking her thumb.

"Mary Michelle."

Charlene locks eyes with Larry.

"Your doll?"

"Noooo…"

"Hush. It's okay. Who is Mary…?"

"Mary Michelle."

"Who is Mary Michelle?"

"She's my friend."

"Does she live around here?" Larry asks.

"Yes."

"Where? Next door?"

"Noooo…"
"Where then?"
"In my room."

47

48

## **Chapter Five**

Dressed in overalls for work, Larry places the two cheese sandwiches and thermos of coffee into his lunch pail and turns to join Michelle at the breakfast table. Charlene watches the school bus pull away from the adjoining living room window and then turns to join the rest of the family in the kitchen. A sizzling line of bacon sits on the stove cooking as she pours cranberry juice from a pitcher of stained glass, an antique. She pours a small glass for her daughter and a taller one for her husband. Michelle sits by her mother's elbow, feet dangling in a lime green dress and white socks. The socks had little lamb appliqués which matched the pins on her curly hair. She munches on a piece of toast as Charlene finally doles out bacon and then some scrambled eggs onto the child's plate and heaves the rest of the hefty portion onto Larry's.

Charlene sits and sips on a mug of coffee. "First day of school. I'm glad they're both excited."
Larry chews, studying his wife. "You're not eating."
"I'll eat after I drop off Michelle at kindergarten."
Larry observes his wife of twelve years as she sits lost in her own thoughts. She sips again, stands, pours more coffee and then rejoins them. She places a dollop of cream and then a spoonful of sugar.
Then she adds another spoonful.
Then, another and another.
Larry reaches over as Michelle watches between them. He places a hand over Charlene's to stop her spoon.
"Sweet tooth this morning?"
Charlene's reverie broken, she places the spoon back on the formica table, then takes it again, stirring the coffee. She sips the hot brew and nods. "I needed that today."

49

"Going in today?"

"No, the first appointment isn't until tomorrow after lunch, thank God."

"We need to catch up on…"

Charlene nods. "Let's not talk here…". She gestures to Michelle as the child ate.

"Ok. After dinner…"

"No, I mean, not in here or with her." Charlene qualifies.

Larry's eyes register puzzlement. "Not here? Where?"

"I got a sitter for tomorrow."

"Okay. Whatever you want. Can you give me a hint, dear?"

Charlene glances over at Michelle who intently watches. "Hon, go and brush your teeth and comb your hair. I'll take you to school in a few…"

Michelle shyly smiles, kisses her father and saunters merrily out of the room.

"We need to talk, but not here in the house."

"There's no one here but us."

"I know. Well, YOU think."

"Wait."

"What?"

"Are you trying to tell me you believe all that about some people in Michelle's closet?!"

"No…"

"Yes, you do. You believe her imaginary playmate too, don't you?"

"Mary."

"Mary something."

"Mary Michelle."

Larry paused. "Dear, it's a new house. Michelle is just getting used to it and so are the boys - but the boys are older and have each other."

"I know. She needs a sister, maybe."

"She's making it up as she doesn't have one."

Charlene pauses.

"Is this about the blankets?"

"Well, how do you explain them?"

Larry finishes his coffee and stands to leave. He kisses Charlene. "We'll talk about all this at dinner."

"Not here."

"You really believe someone's listening?"

"Shush."

Larry raises an eyebrow, forever a skeptic.

"I don't know. I truly don't know." Charlene replies, exasperated.

"Okay. If it makes you feel better, I'll go with you to the basement when you do your laundry."

"And the bedrooms?"

"The boys' or Michelle's?" Larry looked on quizzically. "It might be the boys pranking us."

"Mommee?" Both parents turn.

"Mary Michelle said the people in the closet took the blankeeets."

## Chapter Six

Charlene takes the easiest route past the woods abutting their property. It was the fastest way to Michelle's kindergarten and also went past the road that led out into the country where her brother Nick lived. She rolls the window down in the mild early September breeze, taking in the scent of sunflowers. She glances at Michelle seated and strapped next to her. In those days, a seatbelt was enough to secure a child and they could easily sit up front if no one was in the passenger seat.

Lost in thought, Charlene pulls up to the front portico of the elementary school as the school monitor tipped her hat at Charlene and the child exited and took the woman's hand. Charlene absently waves at her daughter and Michelle blew a kiss in return as she went up the steps to the front doors. On impulse, Charlene decides to stop by the grocery store to pick up some ingredients and make homemade doughnuts for the children which Larry also enjoyed.

At Inkman's, Charlene steps out and enters, turning towards the cool breezes coming from the freezer section. She makes a beeline for the Pillsbury rolls and then turns and spots the confectioner's sugar in the next aisle. A gentleman in supermarket uniform tips his hat and Charlene demurely grins as she adds the bag of sugar to her cart.

The Ford Fairlane in blue exits the parking lot and Charlene aims the car for home. Despite the distraction of routine, Charlene's thoughts steer her once more to the blanket disappearances. Two nights in a row. The first night, she had tossed it up to her own forgetfulness, though she wasn't as forgetful as her brother. The second night was the night that bothered her the most as she had pointedly placed each blanket back to each child's bed. She decides on the spur of the moment to investigate the boys' room and then Michelle's room for a secret entrance from outside. Her methodical ways, she mused would possibly pay off with a logical

answer if she walked around the perimeter of the new home and located any
outside entrances she may not be aware of.

Charlene shivers at the thought that there was an intruder in the house who pulled
blankets off her children for some odd reason or another. Intruders don't pull
pranks. They break in to steal, or worse, murder, like the family who were shot in
cold blood in their beds after the famous book Truman Capote had written.
However, while the children were in school, she would first make her batch of
doughnuts to help relax her and then she would do her little investigation.

Charlene eases the car out of traffic, heads for her street and parks right before the
two-car garage in the circle of homes. She pulls open the latch to the screen door,
holds it as she digs in her handbag for the house keys and inserts to disengage the
bolt at the front door. Charlene enters the quiet house, turns and observes the
normal hustle and bustle of the roundabout where her house was part of a circle
facing a large expanse of grass. The central 'island' of grass is where all the
neighborhood children play at dusk when they return from playing at the park next
to her new house. That park by itself held some odd vibe, and had a history of
sorts since it was made in the 1920's. Through the screen door, she notes the circle
of grass empty of children. It was a weekday and they were in school.

The Lemkes only had one neighbor; Rob and Ron's friend Tim and his parents to
the left of them. The strange and foreboding park on the right side of them
presented a place for the neighborhood children to play, but it's mysterious depth
also lent an aura that enticed adventure in the older children. The other neighbor
sat behind their property - their backyards connected. Charlene dimly wondered if
the odd "vampire" neighbors whose backyard joined theirs was somehow
responsible for breaking into the house as they had the odd animal skulls and bones
hanging from threads in a willow tree.

After the episode with Tim lying on the grass, the image of the bones and skulls
never left Charlene, tinging her with worry. She mused at how this house had its

54

share of oddities and how the neighbor behind them added to that plethora of oddness. However, the thought of Mary Michelle, an imaginary playmate, if she was one, unsettled Charlene even more - and when Michelle brought up the "people in the closet", she wondered if they had purchased the wrong house. A haunted one. The off-putting feeling seem to become more and more pronounced as the weeks progressed into September.

Charlene stops to pause and remove her sweater and shoes in the living room foyer, placing the keys on the table by the door. The living room sits surrounded by two bookcases and a television, immaculate and scented with lemon. It sat brightly and cheerfully with touches of blues and yellows in a floral pattern from the sofa and matching wing chairs. The furniture all faced a coffee table which sat in the center of the room, the Persian rug in a pattern showing through the table's glass right underneath. The china tea service on a glass rollaway cart sat nearby, gleaming. Someday, she pondered fondly, they would be antiques. She loved antiques and hoped she would own some when they were more settled. She passed the phone by the wall and gave it a perfunctory dusting with her hand. She examined her fingers and noted there was no dust on the phone.

Charlene strides into the kitchen and cleans up the remains of the breakfast items, files the plates into the dishwasher and wipes up the counters. She pushes the chairs back under the formica table, wipes it clean and leaves the salt and pepper shaker in the middle. Meticulously, she checks and rechecks the stovetop, the inside of the refrigerator shelves and surveys the counter tops for anything she might have missed. Satisfied now, Charlene unpacks the groceries from the bag and pulls out the cookie pans from the bottom of the oven. She would roll the doughnuts on the counter before dusting them with sugar once they were baked. While she slams the Pillsbury paper cans to unravel the dough, the phone rings in the living room. Wiping her hands on a dishcloth, she darts for the wall phone, a princess style in blue. The phone stops ringing as Charlene grabs the handset. "Hello? Hello?'

55

Charlene replaces the receiver and wonders if she should wait a few minutes just in case it was her mother in law who loves gracing them with schoolhouse cookies, a favorite of Michelle.
Silence.
Charlene strides back into the kitchen. At the threshold she stops, stunned.

All the kitchen chairs had been pulled back so two were against the wall on one side and two were shoved against the kitchen counter by the sink. Slowly, Charlene approached. Nothing on the table had been touched. The duck salt and pepper shakers glint back at her. The dough sat unrolled by her rolling pin, waiting on the counter.
Then the phone rang again.

Charlene darts back to the living room. Ahead, the two wing chairs sat tipped over the coffee table. The tea service, a silver platter with fine china which was on the rollaway glass cart, had been placed in the middle of the sofa.

Charlene ran from the house.

## Chapter Seven

Michelle, her hands full of play dough, sits molding a figure in the sandbox. Children ran to and fro around her, but she remained unmoved, almost absorbed in her own world. It was almost time for Charlene to pick her up, the half-day ending promptly at three. Michelle looks up and observes Taryn the young school monitor in her jeans and tee shirt, long hair betraying her soft features and youth. Michelle likes the teachers' assistant, who played the piano and sang along as they sat on their desks in the classroom. However, she liked Taryn even more, who always brought out special toys and puzzles for her to play when she felt reluctance creep into her at the thought of playing with other children. Michelle liked the young woman's company, who went out of her way to make Michelle more comfortable in the playground where the children would sometimes approach and stare at Michelle. Michelle always looked up to find a ready smile and a warmth that she knew signaled kindness.

On this particular afternoon, Taryn appeared a bit distracted by the other children who were clustered around the teeter totter and fighting for space. The woman stood up to address the brewing crowd around two little girls who were arguing. Michelle let go of her play dough and took the opportunity to stretch her little legs in her pink pants and matching pink and green top. A tree ahead seemed shady and she needed the respite of the shade and spotted the Gumby flask which her mother had given her filled with Kool Aid.

Michelle skips over and grabs the flask, as the children and Taryn carried on. At the shadier edge of the playground, Michelle sits in the shade of a bench and sips the cool drink. She wonders if her mother would be coming soon as playtime was towards the end of the day.

The children yell and run around the perimeter, now breaking into smaller groups after the 'talk' with Taryn. Michelle watched as a group of boys ran closer to

58

where she sat. She wishes in her head that her brothers were there and in the depth of her heart began to feel unsettled by her isolation. One girl ran past, turned and kicked sand at the group of boys. Laughter. Michelle looks down at her own patent leather shoes, still shiny and clean, the frilly white socks new from the local Kresge's. A boy dashes up and kicks sand over her shoes, spraying debris onto her lace socks. Michelle leans down and sweeps it away with a hand. She didn't have the courage to give the boy a dirty look as her other classmates would.

Michelle straightens, now feeling a churn in the pit of her stomach. Something seems to be changing in the air. An orb-like light descends. She looks up and places her hand protectively over her eyes as her mom told her never to look directly at the sun.

It wasn't the sun.
A light appears to issue from somewhere near the tree and envelope her, the bench and the surrounding grass. Michelle continues to inspect the area around her as she sat in puzzlement. She fumbles for her flask and sips.

"Michelle."
Michelle looked around, baffled.
"Michelle."
The schoolyard seemed brighter but more distant. The sounds of the children's voices appear to muffle. Across the schoolyard, she sees the monitor smile and wave. Taryn observes Michelle as she watches the smaller children Michelle's age run around the playground. Michelle raises a hand and waves back. She looks at her tiny hands as she had never waved back before. She tries to smile at Taryn.

"Michelle, I am here."
"Oh, okay." She found herself replying.
"I am here and there's nothing to fear."
Michelle stands, glancing at the tree behind her.
A warmth, like a blanket surrounded her.

Children ran, mocked each other and stuck their tongues out at Michelle.  Michelle sat, smiling in a sea of contentment.  Nothing could bother her any longer.

60

61

## Chapter Eight

"How was it?"

"Okay."

"Did you play with the other kids?"

Michelle looked up. "Taryn."

"Taryn? Is she in your grade?"

"No, Mommy. She's the monitor."

"Oh, that's right. She's nice, isn't she?"

"Yes and another lady too."

"Mrs. Windell?"

"Nooo…"

"No?"

"Nope." Michelle vehemently shakes her head as she watched Charlene turn onto a different street. She looked up with a questioning look.

"This lady came from the tree…"

Trees again, Charlene mused. Something about trees.

"The lady was very bright."

Charlene involuntarily shivers in the mild autumn weather and decides to change the subject.

"We're going to visit Uncle Nick. You like Uncle Nick, don't you?"

"Out in the country."

"Right. We'll visit for a spell until your brothers get home from school."

"Are they playing 'feettball' today?"

"Football. Yes. Practice. But we'll be home in time to make dinner. I also am going to ask you to help me bake."

Michelle's eyes light up. "Me? Help bake cookies?"

"No your favorite doughnuts." Charlene thought about how the dough may be hard by now after she patrolled the house twice in quest of an entrance from outside. She found none and it made her increasingly more uneasy at the thought

62

that it only left the boys playing a prank with the blankets. However, she knew she was alone when the furniture moved. She found herself unable to enter the house alone.

"So what did you learn in kindergarten today?" Charlene continued, absorbed in her thoughts.
Would the chairs still be sitting against the wall and the counter when they returned? Would something else be missing? Moved? Charlene finds herself mulling over the events as she tries to make conversation with her daughter. The fields of wheat yawing in the wind distracts her as the car goes straight down the road onto the flatter plain where the wind turns the windmills as if to signal their entrance into the countryside.

Michelle wordlessly stares outside the passenger window as more fields entered her view. Outside of the town limits, homes became less and less, punctuated here and there with barns, silos and an occasional clapboard house.

Fields stretch to the horizon on either side of the car as they roll onto flatter plains, the sunflowers now having lost their petals. They bow like curly q's on one side as far as the eye can see.
A yellow beam of light shines through an open red barn. Michelle points in the distance.
" Look, Mommy! The lady sent me a sunbeam."
What an imagination, Charlene thought. She wished Michelle had a sister.
"She did, huh?"
Charlene steered the car onto the dusty stone driveway and put the car in park.

The locks flipped up and down in rapid succession.
"What?!" Charlene exclaims in surprise.
The locks on all four doors of the Ford Fairlane flip up and down in unison. In rapid succession, all four locks flip up and down. Michelle reaches for the door, slowly touching the lock button. It flips up before her fingers could reach it.

63

"Run, Mommy!" Michelle pushes the passenger door open before it locked again. She dashes out of the car. Her little legs pedal in her white socks, cuffed and buttoned in Mary Jane shoes, now dusty.

Charlene hastily exits and slams the door in the quiet stillness of the plain. She felt herself go pale with fright. The strangeness followed them out here, she concluded. Was it from the new house? Was it attracted to her or to Michelle? Vast stretches of high grass embraced both sides of the farm, a dot on a map in reds and white trim. She watches as Michelle suddenly pauses by the side of the barn, looking up at something she couldn't see.

"Wait up, sweetheart."
Charlene strides forward and steps up to Michelle to take her hand. Michelle points at the barn door, half open in the shade of the sun. "There's a man there." Charlene places her handbag under her arm and pulls the child's hand towards the house a few yards away. Her thoughts that bordered on anxiety and fright, almost yielded to a need to scream.
"Mommee… he went away."
"Good", Charlene exclaims as she hastily looks back.
There was no one there.
"He was smiling, Mommy."
A tinge of panic quickens Charlene's pace. The front door to the house her brother owned appeared miles away as she drags the child by the hand. She thought she would find solace in the light of the sun.

"Nick. Nick." Charlene yells, acknowledging her own fright. She hurriedly makes for the large house with a deep porch in front. Michelle looks back and waves. "Michelle, don't wave at strangers." Charlene scolds as she looks back and sighs, the shade of the porch a refuge. She knocks. "Nick!"
Uncle Nick, dressed in overalls and a hat turned backwards, opens the door with a wide smile. He had a cat in his arms, a calico. "Greetings."

"Gracie!" Michelle exclaims as she reaches for the cat before Charlene can reply. The cat purrs as the towering man hands over the cat with a chuckle. Charlene follows the child in, grateful for the presence of her brother.

"Did you hire a farm hand, Nick?"

"Farm hand? No."

"Fine."

"Why do you ask? Someone out there?"

"Michelle thought she saw someone by your barn."

"Nope. No farm hand."

"Aren't you going to look?"

"I can, Charlene. What's the matter?"

"Just curious."

"I'll look if that would make you happy. Come on in. You look shaken."

Nick grabs a rifle from the edge of the kitchen and turns his head sideways. "You stay here... both of you."

"Oh, most definitely." Charlene replies as she sits on the sofa. Nearby, she spots Michelle playing with the cat on the rug.

65

## Chapter Nine

The bar, a sturdy affair in Brazilian wood, stood several feet long, glinting under the fluorescent lamps of brass and Tiffany glass. On a table nearby, two couples drank merrily, the clinking of glassware and the usual sound of chatter assailing Larry's senses. More couples and workmen enter and join others at the bar as Larry sips his drink, happy to watch and take in the buoyant mood of a Friday evening. It lifted his spirits.

Another weekend stretched before them as his thoughts began to turn to his wife's concerns about the new house he had just purchased after a promotion. It set him with unease that the house could possibly be haunted, an avenue into uncharted waters for him who worked with tools of precision, measurements and testing the stability of structures. His job was more concrete, more under his control and something he could easily visualize - unlike the ongoing issues that clouded his mood about the new house he had been proud to buy.

The relatively new house had all the rooms they needed for a growing family and the basement he had craved to make into an extra bedroom for visitors. He himself inspected it, under the eyes of one who understood sound engineering: A house built with longevity in mind, its foundation of poured concrete; the rebars holding the house's second floor, set well into the ground ahead of building codes of the day. No tornado would pull it - at least not as easily. He sips his martini silently as he watches the medley of workers hail welcome to the impending weekend. Larry felt adrift among them as he envies their seeming lack of concerns in comparison to his.

The call came later in his shift as he was about to address some work with his men about the new equipment the company had acquired. Safety concerns that he could control, unlike the issues that appear to be popping up at home. Charlene rarely

67

called him at work, so it had to be important or urgent. Charlene was safe and the children weren't involved in an accident, she assured him. What she had told him was something that he had never encountered. He felt a resurgence of powerlessness which he staunched with a sip of the martini.

Larry studies the martini glass, the slim stem and the surface of the drink itself, sans the three olives which he had absently popped into his mouth while he reflected. The glass reflected his face in a distortion of himself, propelling his thoughts to what may be happening at night while he lay quelling his exhausted mind and be cast adrift in sleep.

The call when it came, came through the company line, not his office. Charlene had used her brother's phone from his brother-in-law's house out on the man's farm. He sensed her uncertainty in her tremulous voice, so unusual in the petite five-foot-three woman he had married twelve years ago. Here was a woman who was so down to earth and so unflappable in the direst emergencies, reporting of some inexplicable events in the house he grew to call a home after less than two months.

Charlene was enumerating the events of the last week, bringing him back to the vision in his mind he had been meaning to fix: The bones and skulls the children found hanging in the back neighbor's yard. That he could deal with. That he could fix. Tomorrow. Saturday was a good day to set his mind to finally meet this neighbors the children called "vampires" for their penchant to stay indoors in the heat of summer while the rest of the neighborhood sipped cold beers, barbecued and shared the shade around the community pool.

It dawned on Larry that he had never met them in all those picnics and backyard get-togethers where the men talked sports and the women shared baked goods and recipes. All the children knew each other from school and sports. Unlike the others, he had not met them. It had already been three months and the summer's

68

sun had yielded to cool, the sunflowers shedding their petals in preparation for the seeds to be harvested. He noted that no one he knew had met them.

Larry sips and realizes as he looks down at his glass that it was now empty. She would be here any minute now and sit at the chair opposite him to report what had happened since she returned home. He found himself flinching at the thought and glanced at the bar to make a move to get another drink. A martini wasn't cheap, but the occasion appeared to demand it.

However, before Larry could push his chair back, Charlene entered.
"I left the boys to watch Michelle."
"At home?"
"No. With Trudy."
"Good. Did they eat?"
"I brought the casserole over. They'll eat with her and Tim."
"Oh, they'll love that."
"Yeah... and we brought some doughnuts we made earlier. Your daughter helped."
Larry paused. The kitchen with the chairs pulled back.
"You see anything else since you called?"

The waitress pounces over in her black pants and sneakers, producing two menus. Charlene stares down at hers. "I guess I can have the steak and the root beer to drink."
Larry glances up. "You must be hungry."
"I'm starved. Stress makes me hungry."
Larry sat back as he hands the menu back to the grinning waitress. "I'll take the pot roast."
He reaches for his wife's hands in a show of support, holding them across the table.
"We're here.
Away from the house." Charlene nodded, taking in the sounds of merriment.
She seemed lost in thought, her hands warm.
"Tell me everything now."

Charlene slumps in her seat, then leans forward as if to share a secret.

"I think it's Michelle."

Larry's eyes pop out.

"As in Michelle, our little girl?!"

"As in Michelle our only daughter."

"Our daughter."

"Yes."

"Let me get this straight…"

Charlene sips her water.

"Want some wine instead of root beer?"

"No, hon. That wouldn't help me. I need to be clear about this."

"Okay, proceed. The blankets? She…"

"They're attracted to her…"

"Who is attracted to her?"

"They."

"Who they?"

"Whatever is in the closet."

"What's this got to do with who took the blankets?"

"They took the blankets."

"Not Michelle."

"No, not Michelle."

Silence.

"The boys took the blankets off? Why?"

"No, Larry. The boys didn't do it."

"Then who?"

"Them. They. I think she provoked them."

"The people in the closet."

"Yes. The people in the closet."

## Chapter Ten

A gossamer thread of light streams through the window, the stream of dust funneling towards the small bed. Pink lace in a vintage style with an intricacy that suggested 'handmade' rimmed the edges of the curtains drawn back and pinned on the four sides of the four-poster bed. Made for a little girl, it was feminine in an almost ethereal quality akin to those seen in a fairy tale picture book.

Outside, the fall had descended its leaves in earnest, pinning the ground with a blanket of leaves in a chiaroscuro of colors from deep red to vibrant yellow. A leaf flies, carrying with it a few more, ascending in a spiral that grew in number and in strength. Here in the valley of tornadoes, it was more likely to create a heftier variety, gaining power to finally lift and destroy anything in its path. The wind came with a sound, one that had the clarity of a whip-poor-will. It resonated in the night unmistakably as if summoning a mate, but its quality heralded something that meant arrival in its insidious wake. It wasn't a whip-poor-will as there were none of those birds in Leavenworth, Kansas. It was something else.

Michelle turns in her sleep, eyes still shut. Her brows furrow as if questioning something inside her dream. Her hands reach for the sheet that pinned her to the bed, the blanket safely secured. Her small hands, plump and pink with the health of childhood, tugs at the sheet as if to pull it higher and perhaps to hide. Michelle's eyes widen in a sudden wakefulness. She stares at the ceiling and suddenly finds herself sitting up.

Several feet away past her four-poster bed the closet doors slowly opens at the foot of her bed. Michelle finds herself unable to move, her hands locked at her sides, clutching the blanket and then the sheet. She struggles, her legs shaking to get loose of the bedclothes. She cries silently, afraid that whatever was on its way towards her bed would be there before she had a chance to escape. She dare not

72

make a sound. In the silence of the room, she hears the sound of the leaves which had crunched underfoot earlier on her way to the house ascend up towards her window.

Suddenly, Michelle finds the strength to swivel and turn towards the window. Her eyes flecked in green take in the casement shut against the night. There was nothing there. She turns her head and that's when she sees the closet was now fully open, yawing open as if to swallow her in its vertiginous wake. She felt like she was drowning, unable to awaken and scream. Her throat, dry and parched, willed her to form words she could not muster into sound.

"Michelle. Michelle."

Michelle forces her face to turn towards the door as something present in the room assails her senses. There was someone else. This voice sounds familiar and welcome.
"It's me."

Michelle's brows pop higher and her face exudes a sense of relief. She sighs as she smells the scent of lily of the valley, a white and delicate flower.
She cannot tell if she is still sleeping, but the voice betrays that she is awake.
"Michelle. I'm here."

Michelle pushes herself at the edge of the bed as if someone had freed her.
"Mary Michelle!" Michelle exclaims in delight.

The girl in blue and white places her index finger against her lips and reaches out. Michelle sees a hand a bit larger than hers and grasps it.

"Come. Hurry."
"Where?"
"Go to Mommy and Daddy."

73

"Now?

"Yes. Now. Go now."

"Yes, I am going."

"Hurry."

Michelle steps off the bed, her small feet naked on the cold wooden floor. "My slippers."

"Don't worry. Just go." Mary Michelle replies, watching the closet door.

Michelle dashes for the bedroom door, her little yellow nightgown paler in the dim light. She opens it and pauses at the threshold.

"Mary Michelle - come!"

Michelle searches, her eyes scanning the dark room in surprise. Mary Michelle had vanished.

Something slithers in a dark cloud on the floor, exiting the open closet. She runs.

Across the hall, behind closed doors, Larry lay on the left side of the large bed, facing out towards the bedroom door. Charlene had just turned on her side, snuggling against him. Michelle peers from the door and dashes to her father's side. Larry's eyes open and he sits.

"Did you want some water, baby?"

Charlene sits up and peers. "Come. She looks scared, Larry."

Michelle climbs up the bed and squeezes her way between her parents. She pushes her face into her mother's arm.

Larry rubs his daughter's back. "Yup. Another nightmare, it looks to be."

Charlene runs her hand through her daughter's blond hair, looking into her eyes as she examines the child's face. "Bad dreams again?"

"Yes."

"Tell us."

"It wasn't a dream."

74

"No?"

"No. There's something in the closet."

Larry darts a look at Charlene. He appeared skeptical, but interested.

"Did you see?"

"What did it look like?" Larry ventured.

"Noooo… I don't want to see…" Michelle whimpered.

"Okay. It must be a nightmare." Charlene offered.

"No… Mary Michelle came and told me to come here."

"She did, huh?"

"She said to go and hurry cause they may get me."

Larry glanced at Charlene as she nodded her suspicions while at the restaurant. He slowly nodded in acknowledgement. "Do they come every night?"

"Almost."

"So Mary Michelle tells you to come to us when you have a nightmare?"

"I wasn't asleep."

"Okay." Larry relented. "But you have to learn to sleep in your own bed."

"Okay, Daddy."

"Okay."

Charlene tucked Michelle under the covers and Larry turned as Michelle snuggled against him.

"Go sleep now." Michelle said as she shut her eyes.

Charlene stepped off the bed and made for the master bathroom past their closet.

Inside the bathroom, Charlene sat on the toilet and relieves herself. Absently, she examines a small painting on the wall her brother had painted. Trees in a forest with sunflowers in the foreground. She found herself thinking of the past three weeks when her daughter faithfully on schedule entered the room in terror. It was becoming a habit that needed a solution.

75

She stood and reached for the roll of paper and straightens. Her eyes made contact with the back door of the bathroom, where a hook was placed for her bathrobe. Above the hook, scratch marks like those of an animal were evident on the wood. It snaked up towards the ceiling. Charlene touches the lowest mark, at eye level with her.

It appeared to be marks made by a claw.
Charlene recoils, almost hitting the edge of the toilet behind her. She gasps as she looks on in horror.

She dashes out, closing the door behind her.

## Chapter Eleven

Blue cotton flannel swishes: The depth of the nightgown's color dictated by the dim bedroom, punctuated by weak rays of light. The face of a cherub embossed on the headboard looks over Michelle as she extends her arms towards the air of the gaily decorated bedroom; her own room in the cold chill of nighttime. She hums as she pirouettes like a ballerina in practice, her toes naked and small on the hardwood floor. Her toys and stuffed animals watch in silence from the wall shelves, her little tea set on the little table set for four, awaiting a celebration. Her nightgown swishes again as she bows to something unseen, her smiling plump cheeks and sparkling little girl eyes marvel at an invisible partner.

"Mary Michelle, do I dance well?" Michelle queries.
Silence.
"I know, we should dance in the backyard this summer." Michelle agrees.
Silence.
"I like the way you dance too." Michelle adds.
Silence.
"I like to dance in the sun too."
Silence.
"Or at the beach, yes!"
Silence.
Michelle stops twirling and places a thumb into her mouth. "No, I've never been to the beach, but Daddy will take us soon next summer!"
Silence.
"Promise me you'll come."
Silence.
Michelle's eyes crumple into a frown, as if she may cry. Her lips turn down at the corners as she concentrates on a conversation only she can hear.
"Why? Why can't you go with me?"

78

Silence.

"Help me. See. Here." A male voice beseeches.
Silence.
Taken aback, Michelle turns towards the closet, the door ajar. The voice came from there.

"Help. Help me."
"Did you hear that?" Michelle asks in the darkness, her eyes now wide.
"Yes. You must go now." A small feminine voice replies. The voice of another little girl.
The small footsteps on the floorboards barely makes a creak as the weight of the child is light. The steps were not Michelle's.
Michelle's steps across the bedroom, towards the door.
"You don't need to come." Michelle whispers within the room.
"I will watch for you." The little girl voice replies.

Charlene steps away from her daughter's bedroom door like she had been hit. She thought she heard another voice, a man asking for help. Was it her imagination? She was going to check on little Michelle when she heard her talking and dancing. As if someone was dancing with her. Then, she heard Michelle's voice. Then she heard two voices talking, as if there was another child, another girl, in the bedroom.

Suddenly, the door springs open and Michelle exits, looking up.
"Mommy."
"Who is that, baby?"
Michelle looks up with relief, eyes luminous in the dim light of the window by the hall.
"Mary Michelle." She replies, glad Charlene could hear. It validated her friend.

"Go to our room. Hurry." Charlene replies, alarmed. Michelle tiptoes away and opens her parents' bedroom door. "Go ahead. I'll be there in a minute, baby."

Charlene enters. She approaches the four poster, parting the frilly curtains. The window across the room illuminates the naked floor in a deep undefined hue. The hue of silence.

Charlene knew what she heard. She knew. She approaches the closet, turning on the light fixture as she slowly opens one door, then the other.

She steps in, for what it seems, a millionth time. She inspects the closet room, surveying the clothing on the top shelves and then the hangers with little girl clothes in light colors. The closet felt dark and unhappy in the solitude of the clothes. The songs of crickets were muted here, this room, facing the street. It appears as if the room was sealed from the rest of the house. She cringed. She sensed alienation, as if one who was a trespasser in her own house. She thought of the solace of the master bedroom where both Larry and their daughter awaited her in slumber.

Charlene bolts to shut the closet, extinguishes the light and strides with trepidation out of the room. Behind her, by the closet door, a shadow appears to move, watching. Charlene feels her skin prickle, willing herself not to make a sudden turn, afraid that if she did, she would see something following her. She felt it. Something watching from behind, waiting.

Waiting and watching.

80

## Chapter Twelve

I heard you would come. I waited and waited and waited. Something like a sense deep in the back of my head, if I had one. I am here and it's been almost forever. But time is not a concept I can grasp anymore. What is forever when there is no time where I am? I hope I am not trapped in forever. That would be horrible.

It's all fluid here, but I am still here, but not here. I am, I guess, like ether. So no time, not even place or space. I take up very little of all of the above. For me, for us, we are no longer slaves to time. No deadlines I see, no distance or walls to protect me. They hurt us differently. They hurt us by imprisoning us, if you can understand that after I told you there were no longer any walls. However, there is a wall. The wall that separates me and them and those we hope would reunite us with infinity.

You see, Michelle… that's your name, right? You know and sense I'm here. My presence is palpable, almost visible, to you. Fortunately for me, I won't be destroyed by time because there is no time where I am - as there is where you are, Michelle. You are. One time, I was. I was subject to time, the dissension that time brings, the decay that comes with ties to the planet. This planet, among many that wages wars and prides itself on winning at the expense of murder. However, I will get to that later. The thought of my own decay tires me, but you have time and will save me. Won't you? You won't let me decay, will you?

You are, therefore, I am. I sensed you as soon as you walked into the door. I felt your presence as much as you sensed mine; your energy vastly different from the others that have dwelled here in this house. It has a tinge of lightness and a sense of what I can only hope to reach for with your help: Grace.

82

I saw you with my seeing ethereal eyes as you skipped your little feet in your little shoes in your little dress. Everything little that reminded me of my own littleness so it seems just a minute ago. I was as little and also as powerless as you. Powerless in that inconceivable way that mattered little as my littleness amounted to being doted upon, perhaps loved (As I never did figure out if I was loved), but cared for by a mother like yours in some ways. In some ways different. At least I had that. I had a mother. But I was powerless because as I grew to a man, but then I was and remained, naive. My flaw. My vanity and pride which got in the way of my living - and ultimately, surviving. I didn't see the evil coming. However, it's too late to fix that. Now I just have you.

I also had a father. In a fashion of parenting, of being one who shared his seed in my creation, yes. In other ways of being a father, no. I'm sorry, little girl. I won't burden you with my life or what was in my last lifetime.

I came out of the closet, then hid when she came. She came like flowers - fresh and scented, reminding me of my youth when I courted ladies in taffeta dresses, their corsets hard to the touch past their blouses and small waists. She was an image to me of a woman I once beheld and touched as I was on fire with passion. To have a body is to experience passion, pain and disease. I only wanted the former, not the latter.

Dear girl, I didn't touch her. I felt her stalwart sense of purpose and her determination to make everything right for you. I distanced myself from your protector and she is and will always be. All the way down to how she tucked you and your brothers in blankets. Protector. However, please bear with me as I am mischievous. I now confess and must confess, so that you may consider me for grace. I folded them neatly as neatly as I could with my mind. My mind because that is all I have left with my memories and my emotions. He got rid of my body before I had time to think. Truly, I didn't mean to touch her, but I was consumed by passion. I won't make that mistake again with your mother. My passion, uncontrolled and unchecked led to my bodily demise.

Please forgive me if you caught a cold. I see no one has. Neither can the girl you named Mary. She's not of me. She's never been human. Never experienced pain, a body or decay for that matter. She never had a cold. Nor can she. Ever.

You see, like me, Mary has no body. You, my child, have a body. On the other hand you breath, eat and sleep because your body is programmed to do so. AND, you have somebody. You have your family.

We have no one.

No one but you.

Now that you're here.

I have you.

I hope in you.

I will wait. Until you've grown.

84

## **Chapter Thirteen**

## **1984**

A creak. Suddenly, Michelle felt herself buoyant, lifted. The ceiling, a cream-colored affair with tiled markings, appears close a mere feet from her nose. Michelle reaches up and realizes she's awake as her fingers touch the whitewashed ceiling. She gasps in surprise.

Befuddlement ensues as Michelle reaches down beneath her and feels… nothing. She slowly turns her body and sees her bed beneath her as she lay suspended several feet over the mattress. She screams, but nothing issues from her lips.

Locked in a dream? Another nightmare? Then a fleeting feeling of nothingness approaches. As if she had become a feather, blowing weightless over space. Is that what it means to sleepwalk? She recalls her father's conclusion long ago that she and her brothers were sleepwalking when the blankets mysteriously disappeared from their beds long ago…

Suddenly, another creak, and she plummets. From weightlessness to weight, all one hundred and ten pounds of her. Her wavy hair, long and parted, cascades across the bed as she feels the mattress yield to her torso, the brass headboard creaking in reply. She feels herself now fully awake. She inhales, assesses her surroundings and concludes in the silence of the night the depth and breadth of her brother's former bedroom, now hers after years of nightmares from the entity who summoned her from the childhood closet. Relief assails her features as she hears the comforting tick of the clock near the bed, the lamp with the framed photo of Duran Duran and the posters of the Eagles surrounding her bed.

86

Michelle turns in bed to face the clock, its sordid hands proclaiming the early hour before morning. The witching hour of three voided by the thirty three of three thirty three. Angelic numbers: Three, three, three. She recalls her childhood days when her nightmares began, summoned by a force issuing from the closet when they first moved into the house. Then, the entity Mary Michelle and the magical nights when she danced with the child whom she later felt was her angel. A spirit of protection who sent her to her parents' room when the closet "monster" evinced its presence in a plea for help. Michelle was much too young to understand and his presence provoked fear at her delicate age.

Lying awake, Michelle felt relief that her oldest brother Rob had moved out. She misses him and the daily jokes and bantering they shared living under their parents' roof together, however, his move meant she could have his room. The closet that led to nightmares as a child and later on with visits from her angelic friend Mary Michelle whose efforts to protect her saved her from nightmares. Mary Michelle's visits ended once she had moved from the former bedroom.

Mary Michelle's last visit the week before she finally moved all her things out of the room was not just the end of an era of her childhood, but a signal that she now could fully understand her access to a netherworld. The power of seeing past what others see, to hear what others could not hear, was an astounding, if not an unsettling revelation to Michelle. With Mary Michelle's departure that coincided with her own departure from the childhood room, was an awakening of her ability as a seer and the acceptance of it.

Michelle's second sight, hidden from view in everyday life, was both a curse and a blessing to her as a teen. While it allowed her to discern the motive of others she would not otherwise be privy to, she also felt apprehensive about sharing any of her knowledge for fear that it would bely an ability no one would understand or welcome. Her friends, she knew, would shun her as a strange and odd young lady and that would be the end. For Michelle, the burden of her gift as her mother would call it, would have to remain hidden and a secret from those who couldn't and wouldn't understand given the times.

It had been a while for Michelle since her eighth year when the sounds of the upstairs bedroom and the stealthy footsteps and voices finally ceased. With Ron finally off to university and Rob's departure from the home soon after, Michelle found more time to reflect on the past decade of her life and how her friends had become like sisters to her. How much could she divulge? Would they continue to welcome her as before? Boys began to notice her walk, her presence in the school cafeteria and around town when she went to the movies and saw her friends. Would that cease if talk around town reached their ears? A girl given to hearing the dead, speaking of things that were yet to happen and touching objects for impressions left over by deceased owners?

Michelle's growing awareness of her differences that stood in sharp contrast to girls her age distanced her from others like an invisible shield she was reluctant to break. Just like any teenager forming bonds and seeking to belong, Michelle's angst over being discovered came to a head one particular night when she returned from a night out with friends.

Fully awake now from her daydreams, Michelle yielded to the first rays of the sun and finally planted her foot into her fluffy slippers. The alarm went off to strains of Culture Club. She reaches for the volume to shut the dial off and steps out into the hall bath across from the washer and dryer. It was Friday and Michelle looked forward to the end of the week which signaled a night out driving around and seeing perhaps a movie with her friends.

The day went by uneventfully as Michelle stepped off the yellow school bus a block from the house which faced the circle of lawn. Michelle passed the small park near their house and reminisced about the willow tree in the back lawn. She recalls her father finally crossing the lawn one afternoon, a Sunday, to talk to the

88

neighbors behind them. She chuckles as the memory of the name her childhood neighbors had called them: vampires.

Larry had knocked and waited for several minutes at the threshold of the humble but well-kept home just yards away from their backyard. Michelle could still see the bones and skulls as they swung in eeriness to the breeze, as if awaiting a perpetual Halloween. Her father had grown impatient and was just about to leave when finally the front door had opened to a man dressed warmly in a sweater and jeans, wearing colorful suspenders that belied his reputation as a vampire. He had invited her father in with a warm smile and his wife had received him with coffee and cookies. She noted her father's lighter step as he edged his way home with an armful of cookies on a plate, heaped high and still warm a few hours later.

The next day, the bones the man's children had hung, with the plastic skulls were gone. However, the aura of wrongness remained despite the removal of the odd menagerie. The bones and skulls which the man explained his own children had hung at the advice of a long-forgotten friend for protection were gone. Nevertheless, the neighborhood children avoided the tree and Michelle realized an entity guarded it and lived within despite the talismans.

As Michelle made her way inside the house, she quickly changed to jeans and a favorite tee shirt, fixing her hair and placing dangling earrings. Tonight was a hang out night at the Two Floors Restaurant, a casual bar that had become a favorite in the town. It was an old historical building as the rest were in the downtown area of Leavenworth. She had some favorites and she and Cheryl as well as Stella and Kim would order their favorite appetizers: nachos and guacamole. Piled high on a large platter, they would share it and giggle as they gossiped about the week's events and the "hot item" of who was dating who and which boy was which.

Michelle loved listening to the jokes and the banter of her friends as they went through the list of boys in their classes. It was way after midnight by the time she returned home. Weary, but unable to sleep after all the activity from the night out,

Michelle decides to relax in front of the television. She removes her sandals, padding softly in her bare feet towards the sofa. The silence announced her parents weren't home yet from their own night out. She had the house to herself and reached for the remote.

As the soft sounds of voices emanate from the television, Michelle turns her eyes from the set. In the hall by the foyer, she senses movement by the stairs leading up to the landing which sat adjacent to her old bedroom. She wonders about how the room would feel now, several years later, as she only entered it by day and not at night.

Her thoughts drifted as the susurrus of the television chatter failed to engage her attention. She wonders if the closet remained active after all the years that it remained empty, save for an occasional daytime visit when she would retrieve something, she had not been in the childhood room at night. The family now used it as a storage room of sorts, only in daytime would she dare venture in and dare not linger longer than was necessary.

"Michelle, help us."

Michelle blinks from her reverie and sits up. She reaches for the remote and glances at the television. The anchorman on the midnight news was signing off, smiling as if in anticipation of going home for the night.

A commercial comes on with a tune.

"Michelle, help. Help us."

A tinge of anxiety reaches Michelle's psyche. She mutes the volume on the remote. A sense of disquiet assails her as if she was suspended in time.

"Michelle."

90

Michelle stands and surveys the room. She senses the temperature had changed, sending the hairs on her bare arms standing on end.

They had returned. That familiar voice from her childhood now knows her by name.

91

## **Chapter Fourteen**

I knew you could still hear me. Please. Hear me. Please. You're sixteen now and there's two of us here. I know you would understand. I am pleading. Before you move out of this house and are lost to us forever, please hear me.

I guess I should try to explain what placed me (and her) in this predicament. I know I frightened you: Stealing out into the night of your bedroom, fleeing the miserable prison of a closet and trying to make you hear. That girl Mary could have told you, but she - she didn't. Instead, she sent you running to the confines and slumber of your parents' bedroom, making me more a monster than I really am. I am not that bad. You see, Mary Michelle, your angel, was wrong. I am truly not that bad. We're all imperfect in our own ways, large and small. Like the old Christian venial sins and mortal sins. I think that's what your mom one time called it when she was talking to Rob, your big brother. To Ron too. Mortal and venial sins.

I need to explain. When Mary came to rescue you from us, me in particular, for I am the one with the mortal sin, I just had to try harder. Hard as I try to reach you, you fled before I could explain what happened to me and that was very sad, made me angry and even vengeful. But I can't harbor those feelings for it may manifest in a nasty way towards you and even your parents.
But one day... I followed your mom down the stairs and decided in the heat of day to try something that would awaken her.

It was very difficult for me in my vibration, my status, to show things and make myself felt in the heat of the sun. I am, in a fashion, like the neighbors your friends in childhood cautioned you about. A vampire. In a fashion, I am because I only really, really, can find it for some reason EASIER to come out at night. I guess that's just what happens when one is bonded to the dark. Stuck in the dark. One with the dark... after what I did to her.

93

Dear Michelle, I don't want to stay with the dark or be one with the dark despite what I did. I feel the evilness in me much stronger after what I did to that woman, that girl who was your age of sixteen. Something taunted me to taunt her and flirt and it got out of hand. So now the something took me when my father took my life, discovering what I had done to her. My dad and I are in this place of sorrow and regret together, but he's in some spot that's better than mine, I'm told. Dad can see me, but I can't see him. He is in a fashion protected by a higher level of knowing. He could roam and return to the planet, I'm told, while I myself am locked in a box. In a figurative box that manifests in physical time as your childhood room, your closet.

However, that one day, I broke free. I roamed your house, following your mom, but not out the door. I saw you in your school dress and stockings. The something that led me to do what I did to that girl long ago was taunting me and tempting me again, but now I knew better. But I cannot leave this house. I have been held back and only YOU have the key.

Then, while your mom was out, I came out to play, moving chairs around to get the attention I know I deserve. At least your attention, through your mom. So pretty she is, this mother called Charlene. So neat, so meticulous, so industrious. I just had to get her to stop for a minute to see she wasn't alone in the house even in the sunlight.

I scared her. Charlene in her pretty and slim pants and blouse, so fresh and so young to have three children. Everything is going so right like my life at one time before the something that matched my internal oddness and took hold of me and tempted me to…

Well, that's done now. I can't turn back time and undo what I'd done to her. BUT, I can try to reach you and scare your mom to tell your dad. Then, eventually,

94

you'll hear about it.  But you didn't because you were too young.  Your ears would be too young for that.  Like Mary Michelle, your parents protected you.

BUT I know you know.  I know deep within your soul you, Michelle, KNEW there was something quite edgy, odd and even sinister about the house.  You know and I know the blankets weren't moved by Mary Michelle, nor were the chairs in the kitchen or the living room.

That was all us.  Me and the girl I murdered.  Yes.  I took a liking to her and one day...

Wait.  You moved into the basement.  If I could go to the kitchen and the living room, don't you think I could go down to the basement?

Who do you think hugged you and raised you all the way up to the ceiling, my dear?

## Chapter Fifteen

## Michelle

The room appeared the same as the day I left it, with the exception here and there of some new furniture from my grandmother's house. On one corner there was a hope chest and a matching dresser from her old bedroom. I meant, because she had passed and we had to clean and put her house up for sale. The lace curtains that sheltered me in my childhood bed were gone, replaced by a more neutral color meant for any house guest who chose to visit from far away. The wall shelves still held some of my stuffed toys and paraphernalia, bringing back memories of my old self and Mary Michelle. By day, they stared back with dullness like old clothes awaiting to be tossed; by night, they held a pregnant vibe of loneliness only I would know.

They say that when we enter places of our childhood, we leave an imprint of ourselves behind, so that what remained of our old selves welcome that part of us that now is. A familiar sunlight shone during the day, bringing me home in the comfort of memory and the scents of my childhood. I see me in my mind's eye, a visage of a child at play in the most carefree but shy way, in the part of my hair and in the shine of my eyes. That part of me that is no longer as I was; no longer as shy nor naive as I stepped into the brightness of knowing.

Tonight as I entered the same room filled with memories, I seized the moments I treasured with Mary Michelle. The laughter, the comfort of a companion close in age, the comfort of a protector - and the dancing we made on the wooden floor in celebration of our friendship. I seized the gaiety with both hands, holding on to a memory as sharp as yesterday of an invisible friend who never lived as a human. I saw her in the first rays of a harvest moon, the pallor of the cold bare floor and in the scintillating night of stars.

However, not a few minutes have passed and I in reverie and nostalgia shifted awareness to a gnawing pang of foreboding. Immediately to my left, in the internal compass of my psyche, I detect a presence in the room. A vestige of anxiety gripped me in my tracks and signaled me to back out. It was no longer Mary Michelle who forbade me to go forward or remain in the room. It was my own psyche, my subconscious, now developed in the keen welter of a developing seer.

It was the entity of a man.

His voice issued like the whistle of a predator in stealth, seeking fresh prey as it would in the shelter of night. "Michelle. You're back."

I touched the gold crucifix under the thin cloth of my blouse and tugged to reveal the chain and the symbol I so heavily leaned on. In the wake of the tide which threatened to sweep me into the abysmal sanctity of the unclean and unholy, I murmured a prayer. I knew the voice belonged to one who had been disembodied long ago before I was born. Disembodied after his own actions led to the untimely disembodiment of someone, his victim, who now rode the abyss with him, locked in an embrace of tragedy.

I felt the warmth of the crucifix within my fingers as I grasp for faith and hoped for an answer. I felt I had lost my faith.

While I waited, I sensed his inequity like a spirit soaring only within the limits of lesser gods; his flight low to the ground, loaded by lust and deception. The vagaries of remorse cloaked him unevenly, the desire still burning within his bodiless loins, suffering the torment of the violent and the violated. I yearned to free his victim of her untimely death and sadness, but first I must free him.

However, his lust, rising from his internal turmoil and struggle with something primitive and dark pushes me away. He was not ready. I read through him in the dim solitude of the room, the scent of decay pervasive as the day he hid the body of the girl. He who was without remorse now seeking my solace by freeing his spirit to the firmament was not ready.

I made my way out of the room with regret and a forgiveness to the man's soul for his inequity, but my sadness was more for the victim than for the stranger who gave in to his thirst.

Her name was Clementine. She was sixteen years old like me.

One day, I would free her as I would free others. Today was not that day. I fled from the room in tears.

99

# Chapter Sixteen

The park, unlike a national park, didn't stretch for miles. It was a neighborhood county park. It had within it, jungle gyms, a set of sturdy swings and a bandshell of sorts made of stone columns and an oval roof of the same cement. Bands played there for the town; stopping to play for the large neighborhood who anticipated the end of a parade at the bandshell. Picnickers often laid their foodstuffs, barbecued on portable grills and luxuriated in the lazy midwestern summers under leafy trees that grew high despite the winds.

As the band played, children ran around in the grip of carefree play while their parents chatted and ate; lovers stared into each others' eyes and friends like Michelle's group of teens hung out to people-watch and talk the talk of lifetime friends. Adjacent to the park sits the public pool. It was a place of sunshine and smiles as children, their parents and friends of friends, especially teens, hung out in the summer. The merriment by day, once abandoned to dusk, didn't extend to night. The blue serenity of the pool turned obsidian like the eye of a serpent and no longer mirrored the reflection of the surrounding landscape.

It was within this park, ordinary, obscure and nondescript as it was, where Michelle first discovers her ability to discern spirits in a way that clued her it was more developed than anyone she knew so far. The experience unsettles her nerves, pushing the limits of her adolescence which simultaneously battled for identity and a need to belong as most teens do.
It was late one evening, as Michelle visits with her best friend Tracey at the sister's house and dusk fell, that they decided to catch fireflies. The little group wandered to the side yard which connected to the park just yards away.

Abandoned by dusk where only the swings and the trees witness the progress of the nocturnal at nightfall, Michelle strays towards the wooded area, passing the

101

tree line in quest of lightning bugs. The deepening silence that permeated the gloom of the forest canopy signaled her detachment from her friend and the girl's sister. As Michelle wends her way through the branches and the unfathomable gloom, the glow of a light became stronger with every step.

Michelle's attention drew her to a spot past a blackberry bush where there appeared to be a cluster of fireflies. Her eyes drawn to the light, Michelle forages her way towards the copse of trees, a large jar with the lid open in her hands. Like a small child, she was determined to share the prize with her two older brothers when they visited from college. It was a pastime that she as a timid child didn't engage in for she was reluctant to unwittingly stumble upon the older children who played rough and would taunt for the mere pleasure of it. She found herself enthralled by the light and mesmerized, she continues her approach.

As Michelle edges closer to inspect, the light appeared to be flamelike. Awestruck, she wonders if the bushes had caught fire, but her keen sense of smell yields a different conclusion. The closer she got, the more puzzling the light became. It appeared as a flame without the smoke nor scent that would normally accompany it.

Stupefied, a cautionary feeling pervades Michelle's psyche and she slowly backs away. She finds herself tempted to touch it. Michelle struggles, then finally turns and walks away, watching the flames as her instincts compel her return to her friend and the sister. In the recesses of her psyche, she senses a benign light, although strange, appeared nonthreatening. She gave in to the instinct of an adolescent and steps back, unable to fathom which internal compass to trust in her novice mind. Back to the yard she went.

Michelle approaches her companions with the intention of showing them what she had seen, but the light was obviously visible within their line of sight. To her, even from a distance, the glow of the light was in plain sight especially in the gloaming. She stops to watch if either friend would comment on the flames. To her

102

consternation, their expressions remained calm and composed. She blinks to clear her eyes, but the light remained fixed in the distance as when she approached it.

"You see anything strange over there?" Michelle asks her friend.
"Huh?"
"There." She turns Tracey's head to face the anomaly. Tracey's sister Gwen follows their line of sight.
"Hmmm… trees." Tracey replies.
"What is it?" Gwen prods Michelle as she walks up to the two.
"I saw… it's there." Michelle offers in surprise.
The light exudes a brightness as a lantern inside a tent.
The two girls look, then look again, glancing back at Michelle with a look of perplexity.

Discomfited, Michelle announces that she is going home.
"Did I do something wrong, Michelle?"
Michelle paused, still confused that Tracey had not seen anything unusual. "No, I meant, not at all."
"Just tired?"
"Yeah. Just tired."
"It's early, you know."
"I know."
"You can stay overnight."
"Umm… Maybe next time?"
"Okay. Deal." Tracey brightens, relieved Michelle was not upset at something she might have said.
"Mom and dad might be waiting."

Michelle waves to Gwen and walks down to the sidewalk and stepped quickly onto the pavement. Michelle glances back at the tree line and at her friends who remained absorbed with catching fireflies. As she passes the park on her right, she shivers, pulling her light cotton sweater around her as if to fend a chill.

103

Suddenly, the ball of light from the bushes bounces by her on the pavement. Michelle pauses, thunderstruck. It shimmered and seems to be a few inches off the ground like a ball that had paused in midair. Michelle increases her pace and the light, the size of a basketball, paced along with her with a bounce.

Then, like a large halo, the ball increases in size and began to envelope her with its light. Michelle walks faster, now sensing intelligence. It was not there to harm her. It was there to be a guide of sorts. It was conveying a message to her of its nature. She feels a warmth exude from it as it enveloped her like a blanket. Closer now, she approaches the house, hearing the sound of the television through the open living room windows.

Michelle turns towards the front door. As she reaches the front door, the light suddenly disappears.

"Have you ever heard of a spirit guide?" Charlene queried as she muted the television.
"A spirit guide?"
"Yes. Like an angel. I have one." Charlene offered to her daughter. "You have them too."
"Mom, are you serious?"
"I am."
"What made you bring that up, Mom?"
"I know you. Like my left hand."
"I... I..."
"Indians owned the land. It was theirs."
"I feel like I'm the only one who sees these things."
"You mean sense them - see images of them and hear them?"
Michelle's eyes flutter wide.

"Yes, Mom.  Exactly."
"It runs in families."  Charlene winked.
"I see.
"Yes.  That room upstairs that used to be yours…I knew."
Michelle pauses, recalling the closet.

"I still hear him, Mom.  He knows…"
Charlene nodded.  "He knows you by name."
"But why?"
"Because he knows you're different.  But he's not a guide."
"What is he?  He scares me."
"He is locked for what he had done.  A ghost."
"What do I do with these things I see?"
"Use it.  Use it for good."
"I can't.  That closet still scares me."
"Then move on.  Let them go.  There's a reason for that."

## **Chapter Seventeen**

No, you can't do that. You can't just move on and let go. Let go like I don't matter to you? Clementine doesn't matter to you? How can you allow us to remain trapped in here in an endless circle of agony?

Don't underestimate me. I can hear your conversations with your mother, your father, even your brothers. You are lucky. You must know my father. My father did the most heinous crime of all. Ending me for what I did. I was a minor, he said. He didn't want to go to jail. Well, he went anyway. And the sadness of it all was it was my mother that betrayed him by testifying what he had done to his only son. By ending my life, he ended his in a cell. A two-by-four where he had to pee in the filthiest stainless steel toilet this side of Kansas.

Do you understand my story?

Can't you see, Michelle? I am a victim too.

I need you. We need you. I for one am afraid to go to the light. It would be punishment that awaits me on the nether side. The side where your god sits is not going to allow me in. He will send me to hell. My own fear is tormenting me. I am captive here.

Clementine? She can go. She can go to the light. She was, after all, just a girl in the wrong spot in her delicate life, encountering me, the wrong person to have been captivated by her. Please, help me and forgive me. Please.

I see and hear you talk to Charlene. I see what Clementine didn't have that you have. Closeness. She could've been with her own mom if not for their constant arguments that made her stray and allow me to visit through the cracks of the

107

windows. It was just so delicious when she undressed the first time. The second time. The third time, I finally had had it. I was torridly in love with her and the thought of touching her.

So one day, dear Michelle, I watched her come out of her pretty little house. Your house now. I saw her walk to her friend's house and then to the park. I followed her. I wanted so much to talk to her. I just wanted to talk to her, you see. Believe me, Michelle. I just for one minute wanted to be near her and see her eyes and feel the heat. The heat of her body near me.

Well, it went from there. I found I was enticed by all of her. I wanted to follow her and bide my time. There was a time in my life when my body took over my thoughts. That was that time when Clementine just simply drew me like a magnet.

Then, one day, right after work was done, I went to see her. She was walking home from the high school you are attending now. It looked a bit different back then. It looked like nothing could go wrong. But wrong it did, that day. I found I could no longer resist touching her.

Please, Michelle. Forgive me. I think you must. For my sake, for your sake, for her sake. I am pleading because you may be able to persuade that god you so have faith on to allow me into the light.

I don't want to go to hell. I am afraid as much as you are afraid of me.

Please don't leave. I will try to follow you.

I see it now. More people want your help. Please, help me before you go. Send me to the light with your blessings as I may become lost into the nether world.

109

## Chapter Eighteen

## Awakening

Approximately nine hours northwest of Leavenworth sits an old home, nondescript in its ordinariness. The house, now abandoned to dust and to paranormal buffs eager to experience it's dark history was built in the early eighteen hundreds. It was the home of a pediatrician and his wife. As was popular in that time, the doctor practiced medicine in the home and patients visited his office on the premises.

Selby House sits on the northwestern corner of Kansas, just a few miles of Nebraska's southern border looming less than fifty miles away. It is here in the old neighborhood within the midwestern town limits where a tragedy reportedly happened. Set in the otherwise serene but humble neighborhood in the borough, the house is replete with a violent and tragic history.

The house, named after the doctor's family was the scene of an unexpected tragedy when a patient ended up in the doctor's home after hours. Hospital emergency rooms were not readily available at the time, so the kind doctor did what he could and as a last resort decided to operate on his patient. Eager to alleviate the condition and ameliorate the pain, Dr. Selby administered a sedative and then followed with anesthesia in preparation for what should have been an acute condition.

Unbeknownst to the doctor, the anesthesia's onset was slower than what he anticipated. He performed surgery while the patient was still conscious and the pain became unbearable. Screams were reportedly heard all throughout the structure while the operation was being performed. It seemed obvious the doctor

111

couldn't determine if the pain was from the incision or from the whatever ailed his patient. The patient died in agony shortly afterwards.

Weeks turned to months and months to years. The kind doctor and his wife retired and then eventually passed, leaving the house for sale. In the nineteen nineties, as an uptick of paranormal shows made its glimmer known in mainstream media, the doctor's home, now
reportedly haunted, arrived at the forefront as one of the most haunted locations in the midwest.

Michelle, now married with two children, had moved from her childhood home to the home she now shared with her husband. As with the case with small towns where families thrived in the small and comfortable atmosphere of an enclave, Michelle and her husband chose to move with their children within the confines of the Leavenworth community.

One evening as Michelle sat at dinner with David and her two children, her younger son Jake broaches the subject of a haunted house, anxious to test his mother's abilities. Born a skeptic even at the tender age of eleven, Jake, unlike his older sister Jessica, was analytical and conservative in terms of his beliefs. He wanted proof, despite his unbridled support and love for his mother.

"Mom, have you ever verified how much you could detect spirits? Like, see them?"
"Only what I experienced with my friends' homes and you know… your grandparents' home where me and your uncles were raised."
"Well, there's this place just north of here… and other places too near us…the TV talks about it in these shows I saw."
"The Selby House?" Jessica piped in.
"Um, yeah. You saw that show with me, Sis."

112

Jessica turns to her parents. "It was really scary. I mean…too much for Jake."

"I hope you don't get nightmares, Jake." David chimes in.

"Nah, it's kind of a tourist spot now, Dad. It was on a documentary why it became haunted. Probably to gather some attention to an old house."

"Sounds interesting." Michelle adds, warming to the theme.

"How would it be, Mom, to actually go to a verified haunted house and see if you can see something…"

Jessica looks up from her steak, a gleam in here eyes. "I'll go."

"Is there a tour? Where is it?" Michelle queries.

"Yup. I'll get the brochure."

"Jake. We're still eating dinner!"

"Come on, Mom. This will be radical." Jessica adds, standing to join her brother who is rummaging in the mail bin by the foyer.

Finding nothing, Jake dashes to the living room, pulling a chest of drawers open to reveal a brochure. A glossy the size of a pamphlet sit in his hands. He excitedly dashes back with ebullience to the dining room table and spreads the pamphlet in front of his mother. David leans over to look and makes a eye contact with Michelle. Michelle reads through in silence as Jake chatters excitedly about the house, Jessica nodding vigorously her assent.

Michelle sits back and glances at David who appeared pensive.

"I want to see what I can find out."

"Okay. I'll leave it up to you. Jake and I are going to support you either way." David replied.

Outside the home, in the fading light of night, a deserted street glows with the light of lamps. Closer to the front walk, in the deepest shade of a maple tree, stands a silhouette. A ring of cigarette smoke evinces out of the figure even as it stands motionless. The eyes glint in the depths of darkness as it watches in silence. Just a few feet away, the warm glow of the chandelier in the simple dining room glints against the window panes.

The man, shrouded in darkness,  is jet black and undefinable except for the tendrils of smoke wafting from under his fedora hat.  He appears to have defeated the blackness of night by emitting his own darkness.

He stood, watching and waiting.  Then like a mound of lava, slowly descended into the ground and became amorphous.  Slowly, he disappears and became one with the ground.  In its wake, a dog howls in the distance the peal of the dead.

114

## Chapter Nineteen

## Selby House

"I'm going in." Michelle whispered as her nephew Vince pocketed the car keys. The light of the sun was fading fast behind him as Michelle approaches the aging porch of the house. The structure towered over her five foot six frame, looming in semi-darkness like a defeated knight resting before the next battle, waiting for a salve that would bring it back to its feet.

In her jeans pocket, she had a folded paper which was a standard consent from the chamber of commerce to investigate the house. It had just been shy of a week when Charlene and her daughter Jessica followed her on a tour of the house by day, which segued into the history of the active home. Despite Jake's eagerness to accompany them, they deemed him too young for what could be a traumatic visit. During the tour, there was nothing to show the house was haunted despite its turbulent history. However, the tour was during the day and in the company of several tourists who were eager for a change of entertainment. To Michelle, the home needed cleansing if in fact it was infested or had lingering spirits waiting to be freed. Tonight, however, her charge was to determine her own prowess in the company of a witness, her nephew.

A self-proclaimed psychic at this point in her career, Michelle craved to validate her instincts by visiting the site to see what she could discern. There were thousands out there in television shows and documentaries who made their living in various ways, but Michelle felt compelled to prove to her family that her mediumistic abilities were real. Furthermore, she felt a need to sense the beyond where the disembodied spirits sat awaiting freedom. She would not and could not accept payment for her services, as her internal compass told her that any form of renumeration would end her gift.

116

As with most "attractions" of this sort, the building owners told Michelle she was welcome to verify the activity, but not to cleanse the area "at this time". Michelle relented as she was there to test her own mettle, not to serve as a paranormal investigator who would make the appropriate recommendation. There would be other opportunities to cleanse homes, but only by invitation. The house had been investigated and deemed "haunted" by seasoned investigators and thus became a local attraction to those anxious to experience a haunting.

Michelle glances down at her watch as she enters the dusty foyer of the old house, noting it had just turned nine pm. It was August, the height of summer and she felt the heat of the house blow in like a monstrous blob. There was no air conditioning as it had been shut off earlier in the day after the last of the tours were done.

She turns to Vince who held two flashlights and a portable EVP recorder. Vince, interested in the paranormal, took off from the garage where he worked as a mechanic. He too was a budding investigator. On a whim, he had gone online and purchased the EVP recorder on his own.

Vince's eyes travel to the stairs just beyond, a look of fear suddenly catching his features. "It's musty and dark here." He whispers conspiratorially. He had not been with Michelle and her family the week before.
"We're alone and they're gone. You don't need to whisper." Michelle replied with a grin.
"I just thought it was more appropriate to the place." Vince chuckled.
"Just follow behind me."
"Okay, auntie."
She accepts a flashlight from Vince, noting that the lights had been kept on. However, the lights appear to simulate brass lamps more appropriate for the nineteenth century. Thus, the sconces appeared dim in comparison to regular lighting. Michelle felt it was more for effect and an aura of the history of the home. Or was it?

Gingerly, Michelle steps forward on the carpeted floor, noting the floorboards bending underneath despite the heavy Persian carpet. They creaked against her sneakered feet. Tell tale signs of dust cover the edges of the floor where it meets the walls. She notes a door at the end of the hallway from which a palpable breeze announced an open doorway.

"Let's do the first floor first."
"Whatever you say, auntie."
"If you see anything unusual, poke me."
"Okay, auntie."
"Any strange smells too."
"All right, auntie."
"Stop."
"Yes, auntie."
Michelle glances back at Vince, who towers over her. "I meant stop calling me that."
"Okay, auntie."
Michelle purses her lips in exasperation. She forgot that her nephew tends to joke around when he became nervous.

Michelle ambles to the end of the hall and reaches the door, turning the knob. Locked. Vince reaches behind her to test it. Locked. "We'll try that later." She told Vince.
Nonplussed, Michelle turns left and continues to enter a large dining area with a table seating for six. It was cherry wood, heavy and antique-looking. Michelle touches the surface of the table which had been set with fine bone china in a green and white flowered pattern with purple flowers. Pretty. She touched a plate and dust clung to her finger. An untouched house, she thought.

Then she spots the heavy flatware. Rogers. The linen napkins appeared new, unused, despite the telltale dust. Again, Michelle felt it was staged as a tourist site.

118

Who would want to see moth-eaten linen napkins, she thought. Michelle proceeded further into the room, admiring the formal setting of the dining table, taking in the approach of twilight outside from the bay window.

The wall sconces flickered. Above her, the chandelier sways. Michelle looked up at the chandelier, the crystal pendants blind to the light. She notes no one had taken the time to dust each glass piece. The chandelier sways again.

There was no breeze nor wind in the room. A dead silence permeated the room. "I think they just opened this room for us. It looks untouched." Michelle placed one finger onto the surface of a glass goblet and noted the dust on the rim. She glanced in time at the goblet's reflection and spots something looking back at her. "You see the dust on the glass goblets? Untouched."
"Okay, auntie."
Michelle turned to poke Vince playfully.
No one was behind her. A breeze wafts past her.
Silence.

"Vince? Vince?"
Michelle felt a frost on her shoulder as her senses went up.
Someone had replied to her.

"Vince!"

"Over here." Vince reenters the room. "I got the basement door open."
Past Vince, Michelle sees the door that was locked now open. "How did you manage that?"
"I just tried it again. It must've been stuck or something."
Chilled by the voice, Michelle gratefully darts towards her nephew and exits the dining room.
The open door seemed to lie in wait.

119

It was the door to the basement.

"After you, madame." Michelle quickly turned to verify it was Vince's voice. He gave back a small grin. She was getting the jitters.

She descends, turning on the flashlight. The basement appears pitch dark.

Michelle almost tripped on the top step and regained her balance with the help of Vince who caught her elbow. Glad for the company, Michelle's idea of a formal investigation was still very new to her. Still a novice, she descends the steps with trepidation, but the depth of the void of sadness envelopes her like a blanket. Unlike the tour during the day which had several people and the full set of lights turned up in every room, the feel of the house was markedly laced with foreboding.

Like a wave, the sadness, tinged with despair, continues to engulf her to the point of suffocation. She struggles to breath and stilled her mind to remain grounded. Michelle steels herself as she had several rooms in the house she wanted to verify based on the earlier tour the week before: This basement, the upstairs bedroom where the doctor and his wife had slept and a certain area deemed to be a portal. Just in case, she thought, she had Vince right behind her to verify if she became confused.

The house threatened to engulf her, though it was modest in size. She felt the onset of vertigo and a sense of disorientation that came with the lack of oxygen. She knew it was impossible, this sense of suffocation, as the house was not airtight to the outside environment.

Michelle turned to Vince who remained right by her elbow. He didn't appear unable to breath or even showed any signs of distress. It was her own and her own only. She continued to descend and noted the uneven cement floor of the basement where Vince's flashlight made a circle of light.

120

Onto the cold floor, Michelle added the light from her flashlight as she stood to survey her surroundings. Dusty pieces of broken furniture in a state of disarray, a table with a candle and empty bookcases with cans and pcts lined one wall. Suddenly, her beam dims perceptibly. Vince's flashlight beam winks out and then returns with less brilliance. As Michelle examined the flashlight in her hands, Vince's fingers touched her bare elbow and she whirled in fear to check to see if it was him.

What she found was a Vince breaking into a cold sweat as he stood behind her, his features betraying something awry. He seemed terrified.

"Nihhhhh…" Said Vince under his breath. He was shakirg.
"What…?" Michelle whispered in alarm.
"Behind…". Vince appeared to be pointing over his shoulder, but his eyes remained fixed on Michelle.

Halfway down the steps they had just descended, a silhouette of a woman in a long dress with a belt. Where her eyes should be were pinpricks of yellow. The entity was staring over the top of Vince's head right at Michelle. A sense of loneliness pervaded the scene.

"Oh, don't look." Michelle gasped.
"Nihhhh…" Vince moaned, rooted to the floor. "Noooo…" He remained transfixed and rooted.

The entity of the woman stood unmoving halfway down the steps. Michelle pulls out a rosary. As she grasped the crucifix and began to intone the prayer to Saint Pio, something flew into her eyes. Her glasses, snatched by the wings of something large and undefinable, shatters onto the floor, the lens intact, but off the frame.

121

Suddenly, Vince was whipping his arms about him. Roaches. Roaches flew past the woman's silhouette from the open door above the apparition and into the basement. In droves. Michelle leans down to retrieve her glasses, then the lens. She spots it as a torrent of black wings assail them, her hands determined to place the lens back on. It snaps into place and she places her glasses back on her face only to witness a nightmare.

Vince's arms pinwheel as he attempts to fend off the cockroaches. They descended upon them like a cloud that suddenly filled the basement.
As the cockroaches attempt to cover Michelle's hair, their amber wings of chitin flapping like bats, the crucifix on her palm snaps in half.

"Saint Micheal, the archangel, defend us in battle..." Michelle chants with misgiving.

Michelle turns to Vince who stood pinned to the ground in shock. "Run." She whispers.
Vince shakes, steels himself to face the apparition he anticipated was staring him down. Instead his eyes compel him to seek the relative safety of the open door above. He slowly looks up and sighs in relief as he continues to hear his aunt chant prayer after prayer.

The woman on the stairs had disappeared, leaving the flying roaches in its wake. He dashes out of the room as Michelle continues to pray aloud.

Seconds later, Vince drops one, then two more sage bundles by Michelle's feet. They were already burning. Michelle feels the roaches suddenly dissipate as if by magic with the end of the Our Father prayer. She keeps chanting the Padre Pio prayer and the mood perceptibly lifts. The flashlight, dropped accidentally on the cement floor, flicks on.

122

Vince's flashlight beams down on Michelle. Scratches from the cockroaches mar her cheeks and over her brow. The scent of sage continues to permeate the basement, lending a lightness that wasn't there before.

"Let's get out of here for now." Michelle says as she ascends the stairs.

Outside, the car purred on and Michelle turned to Vince in the passenger seat. "You okay?"

"Yes, I think so." Vince had placed his fishing hat atop his head as if for security.

"You sensed her."

"No, I heard keening. Like a humming woman."

"You didn't see her?"

"No, just the roaches. Heard it behind me. What else?"

Michelle stayed calm. Visions of her previous conversation with her friend Tracey and the sister Gwen, returned in her mind's eye. They hadn't seen anything. Vince this time hadn't seen anything either.

"Vince, there was a woman in a long dress. She was standing halfway up the steps right behind you."

"Oh, gosh. That's probably why I felt someone was looking right at my back."

"It or she was looking right through me."

"That's almost like…what they said."

"They said?"

Vince sighed and then shivered. "I read up on the place. They said that there was a woman - a black woman who fell down the basement steps."

"Pushed? By accident?"

"I dunno. They said there was a portal…"

Michelle swiftly turned and opened the car door. "Where are you going, auntie?"

"Back. We have to go back."

"What… why?"

"That's why I heard someone calling my name. A man was asking for help."

123

"But…"

"I'm not done. Stay if you wish."

Vince turned and was outside the car in a flash. "You're not going in alone. No way."

"Someone in there needs me."

Michelle approached and undid the lock on the front door with the key given to her by the tourist commission. The door gave in quickly as if they had been invited back in.

Vince turns on the lights, dim now in the darkness of night. It was approaching ten p.m. Flashlight on one hand and the EVP machine in her other palm, Michelle prodded Vince to remain behind her with the flashlight shining on the carpeted floor. He raised the beam towards the basement door and they reentered, now more familiar with the darkness.

An odor of putrefaction assails them. The sage was gone. It was back.

"You sure you want to do this now, auntie?"

"We're not making another eight hour trip back here. What needs to be done has to be done as much as we can."

Vince thought of the hot steak dinner they had hours ago and visions of a good cocktail, perhaps even a scotch would be welcoming them upon their return to the hotel. He pictures the drink and then the cozy hotel room where the bed on his side of the suite awaited.

"Auntie, I think the owners didn't want it cleansed."

"I just want to release one who is a victim. It's not fair to leave her here."

He forged on and trailed the flashlight's beam onto the stairs below. That's when he saw the marks on the floor: Scratches marred the surface and the cement appeared to have been re-cemented in places. Chunks of the cement, however, were uprooted by something. He searches for a light and finds a switch. Two. He pushes both up.

Michelle leans down to examine what Vince had focused on and then the lights came on, stark as a naked bulb. The industrial lighting appears to make even the most minutiae evident on the brick walls. How did they not notice those before? On the floor beneath them, tell-tale splotches of cement like a street that had been repaved glare back under the florescent bulbs. Michelle leans down and takes a pen and scratches away at the coating. A pattern began to reveal itself. She backs away, examining what had been revealed.

Vince grabs a screwdriver from a makeshift table laden with tools. Quickly, he glances at Michelle. Before she could give consent, Vince begins to pick at the edges of the pockmarks, revealing part of a pattern cemented poorly over the floor.

Michelle watches, marking the time. Then, as the pattern begins to take shape underneath Vince's ministrations, she smells it. Something was approaching her from the deep recesses where the lights had failed to cast a gleam. Her eyes flicker and tears, the scent of feces becoming more and more overpowering.

Something appears at the edge of her sight, but when she turns, it disappears.

Vince backs away, still holding the screwdriver in his hand.

On the ground was the red and black pattern of a pentagram. Then, the fluorescent light goes off, plummeting them in darkness.

"It's not safe. Something else is in here with us. Let's go."

125

## Chapter Twenty

## Michelle

A compelling urge to flee made me dash to the car with Vince right behind me. I had to see for myself what made it haunted and now I have. Inside the house which we never did finish from top to bottom, was a sense of menace and underneath it all, a sense of profound loss. I entered the basement a second time and that's when it hit me.

Whoever had made the house haunted had nothing to do with the kind doctor. It was there before him or maybe after his tenancy. The house had a definite vibe to it whether because what he did brought in something else or maybe what made him do what he did to the patient was because of it.

Neither of us expected what happened when we returned. The cement floor, in bits and pieces revealed to me that there was an invited entity there. However, not all homes have evil or good spirits. It could be a mixture of both. This one had both.

Despite how I felt suffocated and repelled by the scent that surrounded us, I had to look again for the woman. I read in my mind's eye she had been a servant and not treated as well as any good servant. I was confused, I meant, perplexed by the mixture of hate and sadness that came to the forefront for me.

Then, before I could further arm myself with protection, Vince appeared to disappear before my eyes. I couldn't speak or call out his name. I remember telling him we needed to go as I wasn't ready, but suddenly, my vision dimmed. Then everything in the room changed.

I seem to have forgotten my nephew's name. I meant, I can't even recall as I stood on the cold cement floor amid the scent of dung that clung from the walls what my own nephew looked like.

I had a momentary panic within me - of being confronted, then chased. I dashed two steps at a time to the top of the stairs, willing myself to get out. However, the unthinkable seems to happen when we panic. I saw and felt myself turn back to face the stairs and the yaw of the blackness below.

What I most feared happened: My feet became rubbery and I found myself sliding, plummeting, feet first and then head down towards the bottom step and onto the cold cement. Inches away now from my face was the edge of the pentagram.

I screamed, but there was nothing. In the grip of a nightmare, I languished in pain at the bottom of the step, my neck at an odd angle, my back bent at an impossible set.
Excruciating pain assailed my senses. My back was on fire, then there was nothing.

I awakened lying on the floor with Vince yelling my name, his face a visage of fear as he beamed the flashlight onto my face. I had just relived the woman's death as she was pushed down the stairs.
She, the servant, had died here in this basement. She was asking for me to free her.

In the deep recesses of my unconscious, were all my primal fears lay, I wasn't ready. I surrendered to my fear and with Vince next to me, we bolted out of the basement and back to the car.

I never went back. I was not prepared. I sought to summon my faith with gusto, but it was lacking.

128

129

## **Chapter Twenty One**

Gainfully employed in her uncle's thriving and large antique shop, news of Michelle's mediumistic abilities, rare in the community of the Kansas midwest, traveled before Michelle could understand its implications on her life. Michelle attempted to remain obscure in the otherwise conservative landscape, with its contrast of modern buildings intermeshed with its colonial past. With Kansas city to the east and its flat plains permeated by windmills to the west, Michelle would travel past those landmarks that distinguished her state, her second sight becoming more evident as social media took a foothold in the local community. One day, a woman contacted Michelle thru the store her uncle owned and she ventured from the back recesses of the store to discover a woman in her thirties.

The case would be the first of many that came Michelle's way, but this one would impact the course of the rest of her life. The woman, troubled by a marriage in a state of deterioration, a home burdened by growing discontent, the woman sat at the front of the store, her face set in a look of worry. Prim like the Kansas farms that dotted the landscape around her, the turmoil within the home of the woman was more akin to a tornado as Michelle would soon discover.

Michelle approaches and gives a smile, now less shy and given way to the kindness one sees in spiritually gifted people. Lips pressed together, the woman's hands clutches a weathered leather handbag; her hair in disarray as it perched atop her head in a bun. Michelle felt like lead, empathetic to the woman's plight, the burden like a dark pond on a cold night.

Michelle's smile strays to warmth in her eyes and in her step. Although she is trim but taller than her mother, she stoops in deference to shake the woman's hand. The hand was clammy, her forced smile evincing her growing dread of what she had to tell Michelle.
"Hi. I'm Michelle."

131

"Hello. I'm Julia."

Michelle senses the woman's urgency and felt for her. Quickly, she ushered the petite woman outside the store and towards a small coffee shop nearby. Through the storefront window of the antique shop, Michelle waved at her uncle who promptly took a seat behind the counter near the register. He understood and waved to her almost in a gesture of benediction to his niece.

"Tell me how I can help." Michelle opens as they sit at a bistro table with a window view of the antique shop across the street, the sun casting a glow on the shop windows.

Julia sips her coffee, then pulls back a strand of her hair from her face. She appears taller than she looks in her light pink sweater with blue flowers embroidered on them, belying her internal weather. Reticent, guarded, afraid, Michelle thought.

"Have you seen many cases?" The young woman ventured.

"No. I am new and honestly, your situation is first to me."

The young woman looks away and glances outside the shop window. Michelle sips her tea, waiting.

"How will you know?"

"How…"

"How will you know what to do…"

"I won't unless you tell me. Then, I will decide when and if I can help you."

Silence. Julia looks down at her coffee. Michelle inhales and sighs. People pass outside the glass window, mindful of the day that had begun in earnest as they busily trot to their destinations.

"Julia, I don't blame you if you'd rather see someone more seasoned. I meant…"

Suddenly, the woman reaches for Michelle's hand.

"No, you need to see this."

"Okay… tell me what I need to see."

"It's… it's him. He… he…"

"Who, Julia? Who is he?"

"My husband."
"What did he do?"
"He's no longer himself.  He... there's another man..."
"You're seeing another man?"
"No.  There's another man in the house."

133

## Chapter Twenty Two

## Michelle

Kansas State Penitentiary loomed near the woman's home. The state counterpart to the federal Leavenworth Prison, where the two infamous killers in Truman Capote's book, "In Cold Blood" were hanged to death, is as formidable as its federal brother. Now called the Lansing Correctional Facility, a fancier moniker that didn't lessen its status as a prison, it sat perched on the edge of the older section of the town of Lansing, south of the town of Leavenworth. The homes that nestled there had been there since the nineteen twenties.

The homes were meticulously maintained despite their simple and humble structure. They provided housing for hardworking citizens who luxuriated in the small and secluded section far from the greater downtown areas of Leavenworth up north and the Kansas City limits across the border in Missouri. The humble neighborhood with its postage stamp backyards, small in comparison to the urban sprawl that stretched and dotted the landscape of the county is host to an area rich in history. As such, the remoteness didn't equal a serenity as one would assume in the small enclave. The proximity to the prison, its high towers peering over the homes, tinged the community below with the presence of a past violent and tense. It remained an ominous sign to the guilty of how justice would be served for the unjust.

Just a few blocks past the prison towards the Missouri state line, sat a vast field overgrown with weeds, brackish water where the cataract flowed unseen under the swamp. Further south from the field lay a swath of land replete with thick forest, the canopy reaching heights and an unforgiving lushness so that any plane could not view the land below.

135

As Michelle sat and took in the atmosphere of the place within her car, she murmurs a prayer of protection. She was new to this and alone. She had just visited the Selby House, an infamous haunted house. It confirmed for her again as the wooded area of the park had done, that there were 'things' she could see and hear that no one else appeared to sense, save in degrees by both her brothers, her mother and Jessica. The locals called her 'psychic', a term foreign to her and filled her with foreboding, a sense of isolation and a feeling that something was required of her. Michelle exits the car and makes notes on a small notebook, commencing a narrative of her first impressions:

"After a few hours of conversation with Julia, I decided to visit the house by myself. I exit the car and approach the house. Within the trees near the perimeter I thought I saw movement. An animal? A squirrel? It was too big a shadow. a man in American Indian garb. Then, another. Something shifted and moved up in the branches. Later on, I would call them 'watchers' - the guardians of the land who have through time sought to lessen modern man's footprint on the pristine land now laid to lawn and altered to suit.

I hasten my step and reach the open front door.

Julia appears, this time dressed in jeans and a button-down shirt. Stress lines mar her face even though she was just shy of thirty. I felt myself grow cold, my sneakers glued to the ground with every step. She reaches for the door as I enter, asking me to wipe my shoes on a mat precisely placed a foot from the front door. The button down shirt was starched, pristine and without one crease. Julia pushes tendrils of hair off her face.

The house appeared as sterile as a showroom floor.

Without the lived in look of an older home, the house seemed defeated, tired. I took in the faded drapes which appeared ironed too many times and the formica

136

counter of the adjacent kitchen devoid of decor. I pass a window facing the garage beyond. A knowing feeling of being watched invaded my being as I passed it. Whatever it was, was outside as Julia had earlier indicated in our conversation at the antique store. However, Julia motioned me in a way that told me I was welcome to inspect the rest of the house.

I wander, my sneakers silent in the silent home. Julia follows behind like a cat in stealth, watching my every move. At that moment, I felt tested, as if the woman was unsure of what I could do - or what I would find. The kitchen, spotless despite its modest size, evinces nothing notable to me. I enter the dining area, then the small pantry area and circle back into the living room. I approach the stairs and find myself on the landing where three bedrooms face each other on a narrow hallway. I approach a window where I see a detached garage below. The garage, a two-car affair, appeared in a state of disrepair. Beyond it, just a few feet away lay the tree line and the woods beyond.

A man in his early forties in jeans sits on a lawn chair by a late model truck. Plugged and dragged outside on a television cart was an old-fashioned television set, still with an antenna. Next to it, a flat-screen television. Wires and cables snaked from the garage and into the back of the flat-screen TV. Sounds of an action film was on. I recognize the voice of Sigourney Weaver, yelling "Get away from her, you bitch!" A scene I recognize from a movie we had seen."

I turn to the sound of breathing by my shoulder. Julia.
"That's Henry, my husband. He fixes TV's and loves sci fi."
"I see he likes 'Alien'."
"I don't follow those movies."
"May I introduce myself?"
"He won't acknowledge you, though he's seen this movie a thousand times."
"That's fine. I just need to know what he's going to say."

I exit the back door from the kitchen, Julia following behind me like a hawk.

"Henry, this is Michelle. I told you she would visit."

The man stands, mutes the television and extends a hand. "Hi. How's it going?"

Michelle extends a hand. A warm, beefy hand shakes hers, firmly. Too hard.

Behind Henry, I sense movement. This one was not a watcher.

"It's him." Julia whispers behind me.

"Have you toured our little property?" Henry queries, smiling an uncertain smile.

Whatever is happening is centered around the husband. Something about him has tagged him.

"Still taking it all in, thank you."

"Like it so far?"

"It's peaceful inside." I add. "May I walk out here?"

"Sure. Of course." Henry adds, unsure of me. I sense his suspicious demeanor more guarded than Julia's.

"Suit yourself, Michelle." He continues to smile, but his eyes are steel. He stiffly sits.

"Should I come with you?" Julia adds.

"No, I won't be long."

"You sure you want to leave her to wander alone?" This from Henry, addressed to his wife.

"I can come of course." Julia added, almost in a controlling tone.

"No, I want to get a sense of your property out here."

"Do you want to see the garage?" Julia prods as she eyes her husband.

Henry darts a cold look at his wife. He unmutes the television. Gunfire.

I enter the tree line, curious of the man I had seen right behind Henry. Henry watches and darts a glance at his wife who stood watching over him. There was something there.

I could still sense the tension from the couple, so I wander away from them and the sound of the television. It was contaminating my thoughts. My senses were on high alert now. I needed to concentrate and be away from their sphere.

138

Then, I feel it. I could almost touch him. The hairs on my neck rose, even as the sun filtered down between the trees and around the shrubs that exuded serenity. He was false. He didn't belong to the landscape where the watchers, custodian over the land, protected it. He follows me and despite his disembodied steps, I hear his ragged breath.

I enter the trees, undeterred. Deeper into the wood I went. They were whispering to me, the watchers: The American Indians whose land had been pillaged and laid waste.

The man is an intruder, the watchers said. The tree line was extended, falling trees and destroying a natural habitat.

I whirled, my senses screaming. I needed to confront my assailant who no longer belonged to the earth.
It was Julia.
"Any questions?"
"Yes. Did you do anything to the property here?"
"Why, now that you mentioned it… yes."
"Recently?"
Julia appeared to have an epiphany. "Yes. Henry cut the trees down to extend the lawn here."
She points. Several yards of wood had been taken down, she confirmed.

The watchers, guardians of the land, were awakened by Henry. They were angry the land had been altered by the falling of trees. An unnatural landscape.
"Now that you mentioned this, Julia… it makes sense."
"Oh."
"You as owners made changes to the land. That could be part of what it is."
"Come check the garage." Julia commanded. "It's been here since we moved in. Nothing changed with that." Her tone challenged me.

139

I follow Julia back and found Henry in the garage. He appeared angry, his shoulders tense. He was in the act of turning on a circular saw. It reminded me of a movie I had seen, pregnant with hate and hostility. What was the name of it?

In the garage, I inspected with trepidation. The man was more acutely observing me here. His presence was to the point where I felt uncomfortable. It was forbidden. Henry pulled at the saw, set it in motion and began whirring the sharp blade, drowning out my thoughts. His body, consumed and poised over the saw, sliced with fluidity at the wood, mist spreading around him. I had already made my summation despite his interruptive nature that the entity was in command.

Henry turns away as he tended to the two by four on the table which split and landed on the dusty floor. He appeared to be making some type of furniture. "Hey."
I sidestepped a nail only to hit something, like a body, behind me. A man was quickly walking away from me in silence. He was solid, then turned into a shadow. Before I could lose his ghost completely, he turned to face me with a look bordering on rage.

He was about fifty years old. Dressed in some type of a uniform. Then it clicked to me at that very moment, in that very spot as the sawing kept Henry entranced, that the man was a ghost who had escaped, perhaps.

The ghost had escaped from the neighboring building. I followed him as he turned and darted out. Julia followed me out into the sunlight and back into the trees. Into the wood he went - I watched him as he turned and silently with stealth like a fox began to fade again.

I looked past the forest of trees and above it loomed the prison. The man was a prisoner in the prison garb of long ago when the prison was called Kansas State.

140

## Chapter Twenty Three

I checked on the home a few months later after praying to my spirit guides and communicating to the watchers in the forest. I placed a follow up call to Julia despite my reluctance to return. The ghost seemed to have paused it's hold on Henry, who Julia reported was less truculent and more affable to her. Julia felt her husband had an obsession with the entity who made it's home in their garage for some reason. She was afraid it would compel Henry to do something violent, which I believe could happen if it had continued its hold on Henry.

There were four stages of possession: Identification, escalation, obsession and finally, demonic oppression. Although the man who was a prisoner in life that haunted the garage I would not consider demonic, his attachment to Henry bordered on something that brought on negative behaviors in the man. His influence appeared to change Henry in ways that made him a threat to his wife, isolated him from others and imbued his property with an oppressive atmosphere. Henry became emotionally abusive, violent and hateful towards Julia and anyone who took an interest in ameliorating their issues. I apparently arrived on time as she was about to file for divorce, afraid something would happen to her. I'm glad it stopped even after just one intervention, or so I hoped. Time would tell.

As I sat in the privacy of my own home, I continued to pray to my spirit guides, unaware at the time they were Celtic Druids. Their outfits, unusual to me, later came in the form of a series of dreams. I ended up in the public library borrowing a copy of J.R.R.Tolkien's book, The Lord of the Rings. The image of Gandalf, one of the characters, sprung out at me in the illustrated text.

Gandalf was a dead ringer for the Celtic Druid who appeared to have intervened at Julia's behalf and ameliorated the haunting. The watchers, although still making their presence known to me in a later visit continued to protect the woods. The

142

woods separated the property from the prison nearby, thus acting like a shield with the watchers as guardians. To this day, I can still see the entity whose prison garb made him a marked man even in death and I hope he had gone to the Light and finally paid for his deeds.

I returned to my growing file and checked on the next case, which happened to be none other than a restaurant close by in town. While I perused my notes, I sat in the comfort of my counter behind the register of the antique store where I worked for my father's brother, Uncle John. The job fell my way after my marriage which suited me well as my schedule was flexible enough when the kids were small and even now as they still needed me to keep our home and make meals for the family. The antique store, a relic of the beginnings of the pre-world war two, sat on an entire city block.

When I recall my first impressions of the store, it reminded me, a movie fan, of the days of the notorious Al Capone: The large brick and stone buildings of Chicago he frequented as his mob terrorized the Chicago community. The commanding main entrance which faced the main street lent an air of elegance, if not permanence to the main shopping district. Like the guilty inmates of the prisons around my town, I hope Capone had served his due.

As it would happen, several weeks after my visit to Julia and Henry's home near the prison, while at Uncle John's shop one evening working the register, I found myself hearing a feminine voice. Uncle John had left for the day, thus I was alone. Since the store closed at eight on a Friday night, which it was, I normally made it a routine to bring my dinner to work, eating inside the sales counter at the front of the store. I didn't want to miss any customers who may come in after dinner. With Jake now in high school and Jessica in college, I was freer to obtain more hours and less in need to remain at home to make dinner. David began traveling in earnest for his work meetings out of town which matched my desire to investigate what would be the beginnings of a paranormal team.

143

Tonight, as the passers by dwindled and the streetlights came on, I decided to take a quick trip to the ladies' room in the back of the store where we had a kitchen and a storage area. In my mind, I still found myself dwelling on the visit to Julia and Henry's house and her recent report of the events. I hoped upon hope that the druids had kept the ghost of the prisoner at bay if not entirely off the property. For some reason, the case stayed with me and as I walked towards the back of the store, I felt watched. Perhaps since it was my first case, I mulled over the details, or so I thought.

On a chair in the kitchen, Vince, while visiting, had left his EVP equipment and a new rem pod I had recently purchased along with a K2 meter. Our intention was to go to a new case together, thus I had instructed him to leave it there if he wasn't available on the designated night. Next to the equipment were cat balls which I had intended to use during our investigations, if not for Kelly, our cat.

I approach the office refrigerator, went to grab a Tupperware of my sandwich in hand and shut it. The spirit box, also a new equipment addition purchased by my daughter, emitted a sound. The cat balls lit up and moved. Then the LED light from the rem pod went off. I paused, my hand still on the Tupperware, when I felt a hand reach for it. It was as if whoever was in the kitchen with me wanted my dinner.

I let go. The tub of plastic moved and came to rest at the edge of the counter. I smelled what appeared to be some delicate perfume. Whoever was in the room was feminine. Now intrigued, I edged towards the chair where the equipment lay.

The rem pod's yellow light kept going off, the spirit box and the K2 meter were all on. In unison, they emitted and verified an entity in the room. Then as fast as the scent arrived, it faded.
I pause in wait to see more.

144

Silence reigned in the room. I reach for my plastic container and grabbed a drink bottle which contained my iced tea from home. I walk out, my sneakers softly padding the way back to the front of the store.

I stroll through the store on my way to the other end to inspect any gaps on shelves were objects that were purchased might have left an empty spot. I like keeping the merchandise, mostly antiques of every type, in order with shelves from each vendor filled. As I walk from one consignment area to another, I check each consignee's shelves. Everything was in order.

Inspection done, I dash to return with my lunch and drink still in hand and enter the counter where I had sat by the register. I sat down. In front of me on the counter, lay a dainty flowered teapot. The teapot had pink flowers and seemed vintage, not antique. It looked very pretty. It was perhaps from the nineteen thirties or forties.

I survey the area for a buyer who might have placed it there it in my absence from the register, still contemplating the item or perhaps still in the midst of browsing the large store. I distinctly recall the particular consignment area it came from and decided that if the buyer was no longer in the store, to return it to its proper spot. Everything is cataloged and the purchase recorded for the consignee.

Minutes passed. As I finish my sandwich, I noted no one else was in the store. I stand, grabbed the teapot and walked back to the consignment area where it belonged. The area happened to be near the kitchen, just outside the storage room. As I placed the pot back, something beeped. From the kitchen's open door, I spot the light from the K2 meter go off inside the kitchen. I reentered just in time to see the cat balls roll… and ended by my feet. Each of the three balls were glimmering and moving in unison. The rem pod's LED glowed and went crazy.

I turned back to the consignee's area where the teapot belonged. Something was signaling me. The teapot had not been on the counter at the front of the store when I left for the kitchen. Who placed it there? Uncle John was orderly and neat. He

145

trained me to be sure to catalog and place all items where they belonged every day before signing off. He did not leave the pot there and I knew I had not seen it on the counter before.

I grabbed the EVP monitor and approached the small area where the teapot lay. As I approached, the EVP went off. It emitted a stronger signal once it was closer to the teapot. I pulled a chair and sat across from the teapot.

I murmured a prayer and I sensed a presence who appeared benign. It was not afraid of the Saint Micheal prayer. I made the sign of the cross and as I did the EVP went off again. I glance at the on button to make sure it was recording. The scent of flowers returned with a vengeance as soon as I picked up the teapot. Verbena.

"I have my rem pod in the other room. I am going to get it."
I stood, placing the teapot down on the bench and shortly returned with the rem pod.
"Make the rem pod go if you want to communicate with me."
The light came on. The cat balls lit up. That's two independent pieces of equipment.
"Okay. Is it the teapot you want? Light the rem pod once for yes and two lights for no."
One light once.
"You want the teapot."
Once. Yes.
"Is the teapot yours?"
Once. Yes, it was.
I re-checked the EVP and turned up the volume.
"What's your name?"
The rod from the EVP turns fully to the right. It had registered something.
"Tell me again."
The rod turns to the right. Again.

146

"Should I sell the teapot?"
Twice the light comes on the rem pod.  No.
"I'll hold on to it."
The three cat balls glowed, rolled out to me by my seat.

I stood, grabbed a blue label and a pen.  I marked the teapot SOLD.
Behind me, the rem pod lighted up.  Once.

I placed a doily under the teapot where the pot was originally on display.  I dash to
the register, pull out the large binder of purchases to check the consignee list to
mark it 'sold.'  Where the line was empty on the paper, a name was hastily written
in large ink:  Alice.
I shivered.
Silence.
I looked out at the large storefront windows, passers by hurriedly walking past.
I turn and trot back to the teapot.

"Is your name Alice?"
The balls whizzed past me, rolled and lighted in unison.
The rem pod lit once.  Yes.

147

148

# **Chapter Twenty Four**

## **Alice**

Alice Meyer passed away after several episodes of beatings by her husband.
Pregnant with her first child, she suffered multiple lacerations and finally lost her
baby while she tried to deliver, her body too tired from the injuries, finally
surrendering to death. Michelle went to the records office to determine why she
was at the store, wondering if she died on the premises. Michelle concluded that
she missed the belongings she had left behind in life and after a short life and
tragic death, she remained on earth, haunting the antique store.

Michelle enters the antique store at dusk after perusing the records at city hall.
This time, with her daughter and son in tow, Michelle began in earnest to
investigate why a young woman who lost her life and the life of her child at
childbirth would return because of a teapot. This time she also brought Cheryl, her
sister-in-law who would later join the new team of paranormal investigators. Jake
named Michelle's team of which he became a member, First City Paranormal of
Kansas. It would be, however, a slow beginning for the team before they became
fully established.

Michelle used the K2 meter and rem pod once again, keeping the cat balls close by.
They closed the shop to better able concentrate on the origins of the benign
haunting and perhaps free Alice from her earthly bondage. Michelle replayed for
the team the EVP message which articulated clearly Alice's name and her reply of
'Amen' in response to the Saint Michael prayer Michelle had chanted during that
Friday night at the store. The second play also produced her last: Meyer. Michelle
wondered why the name sounded familiar. Was it in a dream? A notation
somewhere?

149

She ended the evening with Alice, her presence palpable to her. The team saw the rem pod go off and the EVP needle move once again in reply to her questions. What would she and the team hear this time?

Michelle dismisses the team for the night, exhausted. She locks the shop, arms the alarm and finds herself staring at the store across the street. The uniform shop. She pauses as her children enter their own vehicles to depart for the night. She touches Cheryl's shoulder who opened the passenger door of Michelle's car, as she too was preparing to depart.

Then, like a lightbulb in the night, it came to Michelle. She had seen the last name of Alice on the lapel of a uniform. The uniform of a prisoner. Meyer.

"That's the uniform shop. They're still there after all these years." Cheryl observes.
"Isn't that the same shop that made uniforms for the state penitentiary?"
"I think so. For the prisoners?" Cheryl qualifies.
"Yes and for the guards."
"Would they keep a record of all the prisoners and guards?"
"Ken the local historian may know."
"There's antique uniforms in the store, Michelle."
"What store?"
"Your uncle's. One of the consignment shops just brought it in. You were out when your uncle catalogued them."
"They in there?"
"Yes."

Michelle looked back through the glass of the antique shop, now dark. She thought she saw Alice peer back at her and evince a smile. She needed to pay a visit to Henry.

150

151

152

## __Chapter Twenty Five__

## **Henry**

"I know nothing about this man."

"Henry, you were murmuring his name in your sleep." Julia insisted.

"It's all right. I can look into it further. He's still here around your garage." Michelle replied.

"He is?" Julia replies in alarm.

Michelle felt the onrush of something like a stress headache. It had been bothering her days since she had visited the house two months ago. The watchtower and stalwart walls of the prison stood less than fifty yards from the backyard where they stood. The woods that shielded the house from the foreboding edifice did nothing to make it serene. She knew someone less lucky lived even closer to the prison, but from where they stood, it seemed she could almost touch the cement walls that were over fifteen feet high, the razor wires making it more discomfiting.

The prisoner uniforms, vintage and in good condition as they were, did not give Michelle a clue about a man who could have the last name Meyer. Alice's later recordings from the investigation alluded to the husband as imprisoned somewhere for murdering her and her unborn child. Who was Alice Meyer's husband? What happened to him?

Michelle inhales as the couple bicker away, their voices muffling to the sound of the wind issuing from the east where the Missouri state line met Kansas. The street she stood on ended into the wild and tall grasses of scrub, undefined by property lines as it yielded towards the no-man's land of the prison's fields. She recalls amid the voices of Julia and Henry the history of the prison inmates who dared escape and cross those fields before they were gunned down by guards in their

153

turrets. At night, the stark lights of the prison lighted with intensity the surrounding fields and the small neighborhood. She would not venture there unless she had occasion to visit a friend or relative. This case was the exception as the woman frequented their shop and needed her help. She felt the first ominous signs of a repeat haunting when Julia called the day after the antique store investigation of Alice.

"Julia."
Michelle watched Henry pause as she approached the couple.
"Sorry. I thought things were well after you came. He's no longer very cooperative."
"Don't talk about me while I'm here!" Henry yelled.
Michelle's head swam. She veers away instinctively as if she was physically hit. Henry's demeanor signaled an intensity that seemed to have become more hostile than before.

Without preamble, Michelle entered the tree line, a sense of determination to end the infestation in her gait. Her back screams for relief and made her walk almost difficult, but as she straightens her back, she senses the movement at the side of her eyes.

This time, the watchers weren't here. She was now definitely alone. She turns and glances back at the couple, her neck stretching away to locate them. She heard a snap within her head. An audible click.

Then her head swam, engulfed by something that was now standing ahead of her. She was in the middle of the field, looking up at the prison walls. A man stood in shadow despite the late afternoon light. Where did the sun go? Michelle's mind screams to make sense of the rapid gloom that set in.

She squints as she touches her neck to massage it. A sprain.

154

"Did you want me?"

Michelle hears a voice, a faraway male voice, unmistakably mocking her. It was sinister, dark and eerie.

Laughter. A chuckle.

"What's your name?" Michelle commands.

An echo. What's your name… name…name…

Another chuckle.

"You met my wife, that bitch."

Bitch… bitch… bitch…bitch…

Michelle touches her head, feeling faint. She adjusts her glasses, attempting to see who was standing several feet away.

He was approaching.

Michelle, back away. Go. It was her guide. The druids were back.

Go.

"No…I have to free them from this." Michelle articulates to no one.

The shadow approaches… closer. It was formless, like smoke.

"Who are you? In the name of…"

"No - WHO are you?!" The male voice said. It was coming from the shadow of the man where the light of the late afternoon sun yielded to gloom.

"Who are you calling bitch?" Michelle asks in a commanding tone.

"Alice. You met Alice. You and her… the same."

"I am here to vindicate her. You have no place here. Go to the light."

Michelle reached for her rosary, a new one given to her by the family priest at their local church. The silver crucifix glinted in the palm of her hand.

A growl.

Michelle backed away, her neck in pain. Her vision cleared.

Where the man was, there was a black dog of indeterminate breed.

A prison guard in uniform tipped his hat. Behind him, another man in uniform approached.

"Ma'am, you shouldn't be here."

The man reattaches the lease on the dog who strains to pull away, barking at Michelle.

"I'm sorry. I meant, I was going to the woods back there." Michelle points, now realizing she had somehow strayed away from the woods which she just entered a few minutes ago.

She looked down at her sneakers which were now soaked in wet grass.

"Please go. We're just on patrol. Do you need a ride?" The first guard said.

"No, I'll walk back."

"Were you looking for someone?"

Michelle looked up at the prison walls as the sun's last rays disappeared behind it.

"I'm going home."

"Good. You have a nice evening, Ma'am."

"But I'll be back. Is there a records office?"

"The historical society if you want to know who was imprisoned here, if that's what you mean."

Michelle darted back towards the wood line. She found herself a mile out from where she was. Julia stood waiting in the clearing of the back yard as Michelle wends her way out of the trees and back into the back yard where the garage stood. Strains of a movie reminded her of Henry's obsession with science fiction films. It was 'Alien' again.

"Come in. I have something to show you."

"Henry?"

"He left."

Michelle spots the empty garage, devoid of cars. "I have mine in the driveway." Julia added.

156

Michelle enters the spotless kitchen with the formica counter. Julia pours iced tea from a tall pitcher and hands it to her. "I can't stay. I think I strained my back." Michelle sips. She senses a palpable sense of loneliness in the drab room.

"Here." Julia pushes an open notebook towards Michelle. "While you were out there, I looked around the bedroom. Henry has nightmares. He wakes up yelling people's names and has arguments in his sleep."
"I'm confused."
"I wrote that down one night to try to talk to him about what might be bothering him. He was yelling some name."

Michelle looked down at the piece of paper. In cursive was the name "Harry Meyer."
"This is recent?"
"Just yesterday." Julia looks away, in the midst of a thought. "He's back." That's what Henry said when I showed it to him. "He's back."
It dawns on Michelle that despite Henry's resistance to being helped, he was aware of the entity.

Michelle darts back to her car at the curb, feeling her head pound. Something went wrong. The man is back. She was now going to see if she could speak to Alice. Alice Meyer. But first, she would arrange to tour the penitentiary and find out about Harry Meyer. She would call the local historian. He would know.

Perhaps they were family, Michelle pondered. Brother and sister. Or is Harry Alice's murderer in life? She wanted to tell Julia that for Alice, it was too late. However, for Julia, time was running short. She had to get out before Henry's possession advanced to where he would hurt her.

157

## Chapter Twenty Six

The prison looms straight ahead, the field which demarcates the state line, just a few yards away. Michelle follows the winding but flat road towards the prison gates, Jessica riding shotgun in the passenger seat. She drives in silence, absorbed as she recalls the instantaneous and extreme reaction Alice had given her on the rem pod when she brought the notebook paper, torn from Julia's notations, to the store. The EVP signal went berserk and the rem pod lit and screeched like a cat in terror. Alice's vehemence had Michelle dash away from the teapot, accidentally upending one of the consignee tables, an antique in cherry wood from Bulgaria.

Michelle had to confirm what was unlikely - a coincidence so uncanny that her first case would lead to a murder committed long ago of a young woman whose priced teapot happened to be in her uncle's antique store. Was Alice the wife of Harry who may have passed inside the notorious state prison? These same prison walls she now sees looming straight ahead? Or is Alice asking for justice for a man whose soul now attempts to wreak havoc on another woman via her husband? Now Harry was destroying another marriage: Julia's and Henry's.

Henry's personality appeared to be attracting the negative entity, doomed to haunt the prison's woods as if being a murderer in life was not enough. Henry was a controlling man, riven with hate for the way his life had turned out. He was a classic misogynist, seeking to blame the women closest to him. Was the entity enticed by his similarity to him?

Julia, Michelle learned, was pregnant. Alice too, had been pregnant when she was bludgeoned minutes before she was to deliver.

The tour, the last one, would take them into the early evening. Michelle decides with her daughter to exit and eat dinner somewhere nearby and then return to do the investigation so they would be fresh. It would be around nine when they returned, with only Ken to accompany them back into the deserted prison.

Ken LaMaster, a historian and author with several books under his belt, knew the area well. A former warden of the prison, Ken was intensely familiar with its former occupants. On the historical society's roster, he was highly respected for his academician's adept understanding of history and would serve as docent on the tour. Later, he would be the friend who would guide them through the labyrinth of the prison by night. He was one of the few historians who kept the list of ledgers containing all the executed prisoners since the opening of the penitentiary, a prison whose name still resonates like the infamous prison in Truman Capote's classic.

"You're Ken." Michelle approaches as Jessica shuts the passenger door. The man's warmth
extended to his eyes as he shook Michelle's hand.
"I am. Pleasure to meet you."
"My daughter, Jessica."
"Are we ready for the tour, ladies?"
"Yes, I think we're ready." Jessica winks at Michelle to reassure her.
Michelle sighs. "I am ready, for sure."

Several people eagerly mill about inside the prison's stark walls, pockmarked with age and riddled with graffiti. The historical part of the penitentiary had retained its despairing look, as if the group and guide were trapped in the nineteen hundreds. Michelle and Jessica join the group, consisting of a few older men, some couples who appeared to be on their honeymoon, a family with two teenage children who appeared beset by boredom and a middle aged woman who seemed too impeccably dressed for the occasion.

Several large framed photos line the walls of the hallway leading to an amphitheater. Austere formal photos of past governors, wardens with honor and even Truman Capote stood with one of the guards in the uniform of the fifties.

160

Jessica saunters over to read the caption under the last photo of a group of prisoners standing outside in what appeared to be the prison yard. A guard in the watchtower could be seen in the background, a rifle poised and ready.

Ken ushers the small group onto a row of foldable steel chairs, modest and cold in the harsh lighting. He opens by introducing himself to the crowd and the purpose of the tour. For a few minutes, he discussed the violent history of the criminals housed there since the prison opened in 1903 and then went into the map which was projected on a wall behind him. Then, he proceeds with a note of caution:

"Do stay close to each other and try to watch your step as there are parts where the floor are uneven. Some are pockmarked like the walls and some have sunken due to, as you can tell, the aging of the structure. Try to be mindful of stairs as well as they may be slippery... the cement...any questions?"
Michelle covers her daughter's hand with hers which rested on her lap. Jessica looks up. The middle-aged woman who was impeccable dressed had raised her hand. The woman appeared terse.
Ken, in dress khakis, a grey vest and shirt had a pin of the prison's emblem with his name embossed on the pin. "Yes?"
"What kinds of prisoners are housed here?"
"It's a medium security prison, presently. However that's the newer part which won't be part of the tour as it's actively being used. What you'll see is the old part where there were notorious criminals who were housed in death row and other places for solitary confinement. As I mentioned before."
The woman nodded, unsmiling.
"Please kindly stay together. It could be a labyrinth if you're not used to a building this size."
Laughter from the teenagers who oohed and ahhhed in exaggeration.
The woman, irritated by the gaggle of teens behind her, shoots them a dirty look.
"Shall we proceed?" Ken asks the group. The small group stand in unison. immediately, the woman moves to the front of the line.

Ken towers over the group. He walks casually down a corridor where the florescent lighting spanned the length of the corridor's ceiling. Cement blocks, painted over several times, showed uneven cracks and an antiseptic scent that overpowered Michelle. She turns to check on Jessica who followed behind.

They follow single file, with Ken in the lead and the middle aged dressed woman right behind him. They turn and enter another corridor and out into a large room with several tables. It appeared to be a cafeteria or meeting point.
"This area, as you can see is where prisoners used to play cards or games if they're indoors." He points to several hallways that radiate like the spokes of a wheel. "Each houses a number of prisoners - the ones that can socialize and are model prisoners in their time are housed in this unit."
"Model prisoners are allowed to work. For example, they can help in the cafeteria to prepare food, the laundry to help wash and fold, or do bathroom duty. The good ones get the privilege of
working with tools… like carpentry and fixing cars. Some who want to get some education, take classes and can borrow books and work in the prison library."
"Almost too good for our taxes, don't you think?" The woman exclaims to no one. Michelle glances at Jessica. Jessica winks back."
"Awesome." A teenage boy comments.
The woman rolls her eyes.

They proceed to a huge steel door; bolted on the top, middle and bottom as if to secure a wild animal. He smiles at a warden in vintage prison uniform and the man turns and opens the bolts with a set of keys. Beyond, a short corridor with barred windows and another door, heavily barred and also locked.

"Ladies and gents, this is the maximum security area."
"What does that mean?" The teenage boy asks, piqued.
"It has the dungeon where the most dangerous are house and those in solitary confinement."
"Time out." The dressed woman adds. "For bad behavior."

"Yes, ma'am." Ken adds. "Follow me."

163

## **Chapter Twenty Seven**

Jessica felt it first. As she follows the group into a series of smaller cells, a rock pelts her back. Then, she heard it as they scatter onto the cold cement floor. Small rough pebbles, dime size, were ricocheting off the walls of the prison. Some of the cells had been opened for their inspection. She feels someone touch her shoulder and she jumps.

"You got pelted?" It was her mom. Michelle's eyes were as huge as saucers.

Jessica looked around. The other tour members seemed perplexed as she. Another stone pelts a man's head. He touches it and his wife, a young woman in her early twenties, gasps.

"I need some air!" The young woman exclaims. She hurriedly dashes past the line of tourists and into the back of the group, cowering. Her husband dashes past the line of tourists and joins her. "Wendy. Wait."

Ken follows and turns to the group. "Be back in a sec."

He ushers the couple out of the corridor and turns to pick up a wall phone. "Meet them there. She needs to get out."

Michelle watches the distraught woman leave and then felt someone touch her back. She turned to Jessica, but she was further back. Then, a scratch. Someone was clawing at her.

Michelle looked around, confused. Jessica spots her mother and comes to her side. "Mom."

"Something was clawing my back."

Jessica inspects her mother's back. Under the blouse, she spots welts forming. "It stopped."

"What's happening to you?" The overdressed woman queries, eyeing Michelle.

"I don't know." Michelle wasn't going to give the curious woman any more information than she had, sensing she was negative.

165

Ken rejoins them. "Everyone okay so far?" Silence followed.

"I got pelted by rocks." The teenage girl said.

"I did too." An older gentleman adds.

"Let's go further in unless some would like to leave now?"

Heads nodded. Another couple and an elderly gentleman wanted to leave.

A few minutes later, Ken rejoins the group, now smaller in size.

"Let's take this spoke in the wheel and work our way down. There's only three corridors here and as you can see, there is no social center. Just cells. Smaller cells."

"The condemned." The well-dressed woman adds.

"Yes."

"Serial killers?" A young woman questions.

"Yes. Serial killer like… and gangsters, pedophiles…cult leaders."

"What kinds of cults?"

Ken pauses. "You'll see."

Ken ushers the group towards another holding area and a guard opens a solid steel door with his keys. "Come with me," Ken said to Michelle and Jessica, who walks with him as the group edged behind them in a line.

The corridor was wider here, but the lighting dimmer. The scent of the area felt harsh, dirty, heavy and reeked of something undefinable underneath the overpowering antiseptic.

"I have the list of prisoners in binders by year and by warden." Ken whispered to Michelle.

"Great. I have been searching and glad you have them."

"There's a lot. You might want to have some specific years in mind."

"I might have an idea."

Ken pauses. Ahead of them was a set of stairs, narrow and unlighted. He flicks a switch on the wall. Graffiti lines both sides of the stairwell. Grease and an indeterminate series of splotches mar the walls. It looked like an abandoned building or an old decrepit factory. The stairs ended at a landing with a small window, barred and frosted as if no one wanted light to come in. Then it continued down further below.

Michelle hears a scream. She surveys the group, but no one seems to have heard it. Her head swam. Below on the bottom step, she sees something flutter, a black shadow, pass and fly down like a running figure. They descend as Michelle's vertigo passes. Jessica catches her elbow and they go down together, some of the tourists passing them, some pausing to wait for the two to descend.

They enter another hallway and the smell of dampness, dirt and raw sewage assails them. They were now in the basement as the windows showed half the sky and the ground below.
Ken's voice echoes within the dimly lit hall. "This end leads to what wardens refer to as "The dungeon." He walks, ushering the group over, watching the last enter through another barred door marked "Dungeon."

Suddenly, Michelle feels a powerful hand push her and she falls flat onto the cement floor.
"Mom!" Jessica reaches with alarm. The tourists around them begin murmuring and converge around Michelle.
"What happened?' 'You all right?' "Did she faint?"
Ken approaches as Michelle stands, dizzy. "I'm okay. Something or someone pushed me."
The faces around Michelle register amazement, then a gnawing fear crept up on their features. The two teens were now silent, unsmiling. Michelle felt a heaviness in the atmosphere, almost as if she was drowning. She was by now familiar with the onset of some paranormal event.
"Let's leave." A woman says. It was the overdressed middle aged woman.
"We can do that." Ken adds, reaching for a walkie talkie.
"No, it's really okay. I'm okay. Really." Michelle adds, reassuring the group. She inhales and realizes she needed to be there.

167

"If she stays, I'll stay." The middle aged woman pronounces.
They process to the next room where four cells were lined along one wall, dark and dreary.
"Ladies and gents, this is the dungeon room. Feel free to walk about, but stay in the room, please."

Michelle blinks. She enters a cell, Jessica following behind, concerned for her mother. Several people mill about, checking the other cells. Ken watched from the center of the room where there was a steel bench bolted to the floor. He sits, watching over each of the tourists.

Jessica points to a wall across from a narrow bed, a pallet bolted securely to the wall, with two legs on the floor. At eye level, Michelle notices a swastika drawn in ink on the cement wall.
Ken enters the cell. "The two prisoners housed in this particular cell were Aryans." He offered. "The prisoners in this area were gang members, cult and NeoNazi people."
Michelle touches the swastika with her finger, tracing it.
"What would they do about a Jewish person like me being in their cell?" The middle aged woman yells in anger from right outside the cell.
Suddenly, Michelle's head spun. She had visions of hate and anger, the sound of gunshots and screaming.
Her hand stuck to the swastika. Michelle pulls and pulls and turns to the woman and sees a face right behind her dark as night. The woman's anger seems to have provoked something. Something was manifesting in the cell in response to the middle aged woman.
"I can't... Michelle exclaims as she attempts to pull her hand away. Something within Michelle made her want to attack the woman.
Jessica watches in shock, reaches for her mother's hand to pull it away. "Get out of the cell, Jess."

Jessica protectively hugs her mother instead as Michelle reaches over to touch the narrow pallet in the cell. She had to get a sense of what had occurred within that small room.

The middle aged woman, a mirror of terror written on her face, turns pale and moves away, almost tripping on the bench outside the cell. She wrings her hands as she watches Michelle's transformation.

Blood gushes, covering the floor. A man, mutilated so badly that his tongue hung out almost severed stands next to the pallet. Jessica gasps as she sees Michelle's eyes look in horror on the floor. Michelle smells the blood, overwhelmed by the reenactment of a tragedy as her eyes travel up to the specter of the mutilated man. She senses the man died in the cell in the hands of the Aryan who had drawn the swastika.

Michelle recites the Our Father, Jessica joining in. Ken rushes to their side.

"Let's go." Jessica pulls her mother out of the cell. The rest of the group scatter and rush out of the room, terrified. Michelle rushes out with Jessica as they follow several women in the group crying. It was the end of the tour.

169

## Chapter Twenty Eight

## Michelle

I had to go back. Later that evening, after supper at a diner nearby, I headed back. Jessica wouldn't be returning to the psychiatric part of the prison, where she later told me what she saw and heard. It still haunts her nightmares and she wouldn't speak about it further. An entity, akin to a rake, a large spindly creature about nine feet tall stared at her from one of the rooms. The head was on backwards, the knees attached backwards, glaring balefully at her. I told my beautiful daughter she needn't come with me, but she insisted, so protective she was of me.

Ken produced the ledgers with all the names for us and I sensed Alice's presence in the well-lit office he provided. We sat, Jessica and I with Ken on a chair opposite, perusing the ledgers that were marked by years and decades. I homed in on one particular year as it stood out, but a binder which I had not noticed before fell on the floor. I picked it up and noted it was different in color and was heavier. It had the prisoner list on death row. The year was nineteen fifty six.

I look up to find Ken somberly looking on and hoped it was the right one. I was mentally exhausted, drained by the encounters in the dungeon and ready to call it a night and I knew I wouldn't until I had some progress to resolve Julia, Henry and Alice's dilemma.

Alice. My thoughts of her led her to me. I felt her. The scent of something so fleeting, yet so fresh and like a newly opened flower assailed me. Alice seemed to be by my side, egging me on in a gentle and kind way.
This was the binder.

171

I leafed through several faces, all standing for the camera as a mug shot, all in dull prison garb, the number held at chest length.

Then, one page opened and a perceptible lightness and a sigh filled the room. My eyes stopped at a tall man with dark hair with penetrating blue eyes. Harold Meyer.

I pointed to the photograph. Executed July, 1956.

Then the lights winked and then returned doubly bright.

I had found Alice's husband.

Executed for murder of his wife and unborn child during her labor. I turned, nodded to Ken and Jessica and stood. I would now be able to address the entity at the garage of Julia and Henry's house and hopefully clear them of this menace. I hope.

The lights from the previous hallway shone brightly into the dimly lit dungeon area. I steeled myself. It was eleven fifteen at night. Jessica stood at the threshold, her hands wrapped around her as if for protection. She had a crucifix in her palm, holy water in the other. Ken watched behind her while a prison guard stood nearby.

I reentered the cell I had the encounter earlier. The heaviness greets me like I am underwater, the oppressive atmosphere pushing against me. I see the swastika as if it was daring me to touch it once again, but I refrained. I wanted to make contact with the man who was mutilated: To set him free. Pictures in my head sailed in front of my eyes: Prisoners executed, hanging, lying on pallets dead as the cement floor, and women imprisoned because of their husbands who accused them without the benefit of a fair trial.

I felt my neck almost dislocating, my back on fire and my eyes tearing. I steeled myself and touched the pallet despite the profusion of sudden hate and malignancy that permeated the tiny cell. I smelled putrefaction and garbage, the unmistakable scent of defecation and fought off the onset of vomit.

172

Then, a soul, a kind one, appears in a gentle light. He was guarding me. A benign prisoner who is here to intervene to watch and protect. In the back I heard Jessica dimly intoning the verses from the Bible. I felt comfort. The spirit, a model prisoner in life, was watching over us.

I touched the pallet with both hands intoning the prayer to rise and meet the Light of Christ. Something shifted in the cell.

Something was present in the room. The kind prisoner made the room lighter, easier to breath in. I took a strong breath and intoned a prayer as I had been taught.

"Go to the light. It's okay. Go to the light." I ended. I summoned my faith and it seemed strong enough to amplify my intention.

Sparkles, like fireflies ascended as a group ahead of me over the pallet. Gold and silver flecks, like summer light ascended towards the ceiling. Suddenly, the walls were clean, like new. The scent of jasmine and lavender prevailed.

Suddenly, the sparkles effervesced in a circle of brightness, gently up they flew like doves through the ceiling.
The tortured prisoners of gangs and Aryans were free. I saw his smile, this prisoner, his cheeks healthy with the bloom of youth, his tongue no longer hanging from his mouth.
I shut my eyes with joy, sensing the freedom of a soul who had finally rejoined his maker. The room suffused with an inner light. I felt lightness and jubilation.

"Mom."
I turned. It was half past one a.m.
"Let's go home, Mom."

173

We walk away together, rejoining Ken, who exuded an ebbing flow of relief in his shoulders and face.

Outside the dungeon, something lurks and dripped like a leaky faucet. I didn't notice it, but the shadow had followed us to the top. I turned and saw a shadow at the corner of my eye, but my weariness gave it no depth. I was riven with too much joy over a victory and no energy to falter and observe. I saw a hatted man, or so it seemed.

I strode to the car, turned the ignition on and drove into the night. My head pounded and my eyes hurt. I had seen too much. Next to me, my baby daughter, now in her twenties, leans against the passenger door, locks it and gave way to restful sleep as the street lights gave way to a new day.

174

## Chapter Twenty Nine

You didn't recognize me. I am not the model prison you thought had entered the cell to protect you and Jessica. I am not someone else. I am with you now.

I am trying to prove without a double that the prison within my mind - my faults, my horrible crime, my desires which destroyed my soul are things of the past. I will prove to you once and for all that I am worthy of being sent to the Light. I broke free of the terrible things I did to the girl who was your age when you discovered who you were. Thus, by breaking my bond with my past, my karmic debt to the girl who still suffers for my evil deed, I am freed of your childhood home.
I am free. I can travel now and roam the earth and find you.

Then, after I found your new home with a man of your dreams, I followed you. You never in a million ways could have predicted that. I am he who now watches and has chosen to protect you. Like the Celtic Druids and the American Indians who protect you and the forests, I am here.

I need you, Michelle. I need to be forgiven by the girl so that I can fly higher.... To fly to my Creator who may judge me and send me to eternal fire. I need your blessings and the girl's forgiveness. I cannot see her. Like that social media portal you call Facebook, the girl blocked me. She is now in the realms of the good, the Source sits guarding over her and sending her graces. Meanwhile, I am stranded like an astronaut, taped to the earth where I suffer the memory of my transgressions.

I saw that you are now fully in the awakening of your gift. I knew you would come to that knowledge of your own vastness of love one day. I stood aside as you took that tour with the historian, with the people, with the Jewish woman. I saw

176

your protective love over your daughter. I would never touch her. I know better now.

But how better to convince you that I am worthy of your attention and prayer by protecting you and your children? How better than to amplify your thoughts and prayers for Light to help you help the stranded souls like me?

Listen to me, Michelle. I was in the cell when the evil one who has a name in life, who is now nameless because of his evilness, vengeful and hatefulness was there watching your every move. I was there and throwing rocks at the evil one. It was there to distract that evil one from hurting you.

Sorry I unintentionally sent the rocks your way and hit the young man whose wife is now afraid of us. I however staved off, warded off and muted the energy from the shadows of the nameless ones in the cell. The man whose life was taken away by bludgeoning and his tongue almost severed? He is so grateful to you that he too has become your guardian. Like me. Now we are two and more powerful.

I am awaiting your next place of intervention. I think you may be returning to the prison to help Alice rid herself of Harry. I think you plan to see Julia again. So she may rid herself of Henry.
Harry and Henry. Ha ha. The H's have it. H for hell.

Beware, dear Michelle. He that is nameless that clawed at your back and has incited you to anger against the Jewish woman is still here. In the cell. He is now on watch.

I am afraid of him. He is stronger and more powerful than me. He is the personification of everything lustful, hateful... a negation of life itself. I don't know how much I can protect you from him as he knows I am still weak. Spiritually, he knows my flaws and my past. He victimized in life the soul you sent to the Light - so he's afraid of him too, that nameless one.

Be careful, Michelle. You need to find this evil one's match. He is now on alert.

Like me, he now knows your name after rescuing all those souls in the prison. He knows you're out to rescue more. He wears a hat. A fedora hat. He's darker than a shadow.

He's the total absence of light.

178

179

## **Chapter Thirty**

Michelle awakens.  It was too quiet.  She turns to check on David who lay by his side, facing her as she lay on her back.  An internal alarm told her something was intently watching her.  Something above.

Undaunted after the fruitful visit to the prison, Michelle feels herself shedding her fear.  She recalls a sense of lightness permeate her being and imagines a replay of that moment in the darkness of the bedroom.  Within minutes after the soul of the tortured man and another who remained in his shadow ascended finally to the Light, there was a joy that filled the room.

She sits up and looks up at the ceiling,  notices a curious pattern around the ceiling fan.  Something was there, folded and wrapped around the fan, but the light would not penetrate it.  Her neck cracks as she turns to the window and notes the streetlight beyond past the front lawn and across the street.  It's rays, too weak to penetrate the ceiling, only reached the window sill.  Nevertheless, the growing unease amplified within her.  She touches her neck, gently massaging it as she ponders what it could be.

Finally, Michelle yields to the desire to flee, but she knew whatever it was would only be emboldened by her fear.  Instead, she swings her feet towards the edge of the queen-size bed she shared with her husband and searches for her slippers.  Finding them, she pads over to her cell phone, still locked and charging and sees a message:  It was from Julia.

Michelle checks the battery and sees ninety-eight on the corner top.  She unplugs it and looks up at the ceiling one more time as she crosses the bedroom in darkness and heads for the door.  Whatever was in the ceiling appears to be uncoiling itself,

180

but Michelle knew she needed her glasses as she was myopic, short-sighted. By the dresser near the door, she spots her glasses and places them on her face.

The darkness around the ceiling fan appears to be gone. She listens to David's breathing: soft with the regularity of a peaceful snore now and then. Content he was safe, she exits to the corridor and heads for the steps down to the kitchen. Michelle surmises that her poor eyesight, dimmed by sleep was perhaps seeing things in the night.

"Come when you can, please." The text from Julia showed.
Michelle checks the kitchen clock and notes it was only two fifty eight in the morning. The message came while the mobile was on mute and plugged. She made a mental note to follow up with a call on her way to work. Work. The antique store. She recalls Alice, who suffered blows so severe from her husband that she gave birth prematurely. Memories flood back to her of Alice's reaction to the paper with Harold Meyer's name on the roster of condemned men.

Michelle touches her neck again, feeling a sprain. A headache seems to be coming on, and she jots down "chiropractor" on the notepad by the onion basket near her. A buzz and Michelle reaches for her cell. It was still on vibrate since everyone around her was sleeping. However, a text came through this time from Nancy, a friend who had recently volunteered to be an investigator on her budding paranormal team.
"I know someone who can help with your neck pains."
Michelle sat up on the stool. She had not told anyone about her recent bouts of back and neck pains. Her headaches appeared shortly after that. The symptoms had increased right after the prison visit. Last night it flared and became exacerbated by the scratches on her back and when she was pushed to the ground. She wonders, sensing the onset of something foreign to her. She wondered if David or her mom had told Nancy, but she doubted they would.

"You're awake. Thank you, dear friend. I already have a chiropractor, though."

181

Michelle awaits a reply.

"No, this one is not a chiropractor."

"Faith healer?"

"No. Will tell u tomorrow."

"Looking forward to whatever it is. How did you find out?"

"You told me."

Michelle paused. She knew she hadn't had the chance since the case with Julia and Henry.

Something fell into a heap near her stool. Michelle jumps.

On the kitchen floor, a huge snake uncoils itself on the floor. Michelle stands, dashes to the side of the counter as she flips the closet open in search of a broom. It makes hiss and rolls sideways towards her. Michelle undoes the dead bolt on the back door and dashes out into the night, cell phone in hand.

She dials.

"Julia?"

A movement muffles a woman's voice who weakly replies. "Michelle, is that you?"

"Yes."

"I'm... so... so... sorry..."

"What's happening?"

"I woke up to someone screaming. A woman. I had a nightmare she was being hit with a crowbar. There was so much blood... it was her and a baby."

"Oh no." Alice, Michelle thought. An interesting coincidence, since Julia was pregnant.

"What did the baby look like? What did she look like?"

"The baby was still in her." Julia cries, sobbing.

"I got your text. I'm outside."

182

"Now? Why? Did something happen at the prison? You're still there?"
"No, home. I'm home. A snake was on my bedroom ceiling."
"Oh my gosh! That can't be."
"What?!"
"I saw a huge python or whatever just hours earlier cross my yard."
"Are there snakes in Kansas?" Michelle looks up at the open kitchen door. The snake had slithered down and made it's way to the yard, following her. "I don't know, but you have to see it." Julia adds.

"Julia?"
"Yes?"
It's here. There's one that just went out to my yard."
"It's after us."
"No, Julia. I think it's after me."

183

## Part Two:

## Confrontation

185

## Chapter Thirty One

## Michelle

The pain seared through me like my sides were being pulled from my body. It coursed through me like the snake I had seen stealthily following me when I turned my head, at the corner of my eyes and finally disappearing as mysteriously as it appeared above our bed. At its wake was the onset of a migraine headache I couldn't shake. I prayed, something within me telling me the episode had ungrounded me, but despite the prayers for wellness, the pain remained. It short-lived whatever exuberance I had at being able to release the spirits at the prison.

I then began in earnest to look into protecting myself and my teammates prior to entering buildings and areas such as the prison. Reports from cases of infestation around the world show blessings from clergy and the rituals that is the substance and cornerstone of Catholic practice show that entities are provoked by these practices of intervention. The church dictates entering these sites where the unholy may dwell in order to cleanse them. What I found was that those entities who were more powerful resist with vengeance and in some cases, the ghosts are all provoked from slumber to haunt the living, bestowing menace and further terror. I now wondered what could happen if an entity chose to attach itself to a team member.

After the prison incident which was for us a markedly successful venture, I found myself set back by the unlikely, but possible thought that I had provoked something a bit more resistant and menacing within the prison. When I saw the serpent locked in a coil over the bed, I was awestruck with fear once again like the child of long ago. The fact that Julia texted me that her home seems to have an increase of menacing incidents from Harry and a dream that precluded a possible tragedy led me to set her case as a priority. The third most disarming sign was the presence of the snake also in her home which is beyond coincidence.

I attempt to ease my back pain to better address and contemplate my next move. I resorted to the usual panoply of remedies, as pragmatic as David's advice and as down to earth as I could muster. For now, hot packs and the arthritis ointments were by my bedside and I kept an extra tube of Ben Gay in the kitchen.
This morning, I willed myself to shower, change and to make breakfast for David, whose hectic work schedule would take him to an overnight leaving me more time to ponder my next steps. Jessica and Jake would be busy for the next few weeks with their own jobs. I had thought of Nancy, who as a new recruit, was still learning the ropes of operating the paranormal equipment. Alas, I didn't want to bring her for fear she may encounter something more malignant which appears more entrenched than I could have imagined. I myself, now feeling unprotected while at the prison, would not dare expose friends, let alone family, to further cases which may harm any of us in the long run.

I decided to go alone to Julia's house, set to resolve the ongoing infestation which remained despite the prayers and the protection of the druids. Nancy agreed to meet with me for a late lunch after I had seen Julia and affirmed my commitment to her situation, no matter the resolution. I remained hopeful and planned to consult with local clergy and refer. However, it did not play that way through some unforeseen circumstances.

On the way to Julia's, I drove past the antique shop and a compelling feeling came over me to stop and check into things. I had the day off, but as I turned the steering wheel onto the main street, the shop came into view and found my hands turning into the adjacent parking lot. I parked and stepped out, only to find Nancy exiting from her own vehicle as well. It was another coincidence.

"Fancy meeting you here." I said.

188

"Well, I know you were working… so I thought I'd stop in just to chat about that teapot I saw."
I paused.
"I'm off today, actually."
"Oh. But you're here."
"I am, only because something told me I should check in."
Nancy followed me to the store and I opened the door to let her pass. Uncle John grins from behind the counter.
"Checking up on me? You look like you're in pain."
"Sort of, but I'll be fine."
Nancy did some idle chitchat with Uncle John. I thought it best while they were talking to proceed to the kitchen to follow on my instinct. Something was bugging me and I couldn't quite put my finger on it.
I entered the kitchen, still finding the paranormal equipment in the spot where I left it. I wondered if Alice had something to tell me and sensed she was not around.

"So… why is the teapot not for sale?" It was Nancy.
I whirled, not expecting Nancy to be behind me. In that second I saw the figure of Alice standing nearby, smiling. She appeared solid like one still living.
"Well, it seems that some young lady still wants to keep it." I replied, winking to Alice who stood behind her.
"It's a shame. It's so pretty."
I walk over to the pot, still gracing the small coffee table by an antique settee. Someone had taken off the "NOT FOR SALE" sign."

"Who took off the sign?" It was Uncle John who followed us after all.
"I thought you might've, Uncle John."
"Not me!" He chuckled.
"The consignment person?" Nancy ventured. "Cause I'd like to buy it."
"I called." Uncle John replied.
"And?"
"Not them." He added.

189

"Probably fell off somewhere here." I glanced around.
"Nah.' He replied. "It's been torn in half and is in the waste basket."

Then, I distinctly smelled perfume. It wasn't Nancy.

190

# Chapter Thirty Two

Tomlinson's Bistro and Bar sits at the corner of Market and Chestnut, just a casual stroll from the antique store. Frequent flyers to the Americana Antiques store usually stop there to eat and discuss bargains at the shop which also sold books on haunted places. It's apropos since Michelle's employ that an upswing of interest in the paranormal and supernatural came on the scene. Conversations turn to the supernatural after a few items were deemed cherished belongings by previous owners.

Michelle decides to discuss the haunted item she recently discovered while in the company of Nancy who graciously offered to treat her for lunch. Then, the teapot came up.
"So, I'd like to buy that teapot if it's now for sale."
Michelle sips and almost chokes on her tea. "I must tell you that that piece has a paranormal story. I meant, I still am a bit unsettled that Alice took the sign off."
Nancy studies Michelle, who sat appearing perplexed.
"Who is Alice?"
"She's the reason why I had toured the prison. The case I am currently working on seems to be connected to her."

Through lunch, Michelle updates her friend on the case and the encounter she had with Alice. Based on the roster of prisoners and Alice's response to the name of the ghost that appeared to be haunting Julia's home, she concluded it to be none other than Alice's husband who murdered her in life.
"So are you telling me that maybe Alice is giving you the chance to let go of her precious teapot as you're helping to rid Julia and Henry of her husband's visitations?"

192

"I think and suspect it. I meant, I won't jump to conclusions, but if Alice rests better knowing that her husband is finally gone, she could at least avoid another tragedy. It's so similar to hers that I find it very troubling."
"An oppression on the part of Henry?"
"Yes. I meant, I'm afraid for Julia. I sound loony, don't I?"
Nancy wipes her lips, placing her napkin down. "So you need to take care of yourself. Before you can help others, take care of you…"
"I am. I am trying to protect the team too."
"I mean your health…"
"First, I must see her to feel what's escalating…"
"Michelle…"
"It's my duty…"
"Michelle…"
"I can't just let Alice down and keep Julia at that house if…"
"Michelle!"
"I must visit Julia!"
"Get yourself grounded first."
Nancy places her hand gently onto Michelle's wrist. "So please stop. I'm nervous too."
Michelle sighs. "My back hurts more than ever."
"So I have a solution to your back. It's a healer."
"What kind of healer?"
Silence.
"Do you believe in sound energy? That it can heal you?"
"What would this healer do?"
"It's not what she can do but what the energy of sound can do to rebalance you."
"Protect my team too?"
"She can teach you how to get grounded. Then you can teach us."
"Okay."

Michelle touches her left ear. She felt the unmistakable sigh of relief - a gentle exhalation. Then a whiff of a delicate scent of perfume she'd learned to so well

since the antique teapot incident.  Alice was near her, present right next to her - in the restaurant in the little booth she shared with Nancy.
An affirmation.

"So… are you going to sell me the teapot?"
The chandelier above them winked and brightened.

194

195

# **Chapter Thirty Three**

## **The Visitor**

A perceptible shift as Michelle shuffles onto her bed and the pain knifes through her and wedges onto her neck like an axe. She senses Alice next to her as if attempting to support her weight as she sits at the edge of the bed. All off-kilter like a swing off its hinges, about to plummet, she sank back onto the mattress on her back seeking relief. The ceiling fan, white but edged with dust, makes a somnolent whirl as a breeze creeps through the window. The scent of hay and fertilizer enters, sordid, common and dull unlike the brilliant yellow of rapeseed fields.

Michelle reaches with one arm for her cellphone, willing herself to ignore the pain as she pushes the correct buttons to call Julia. She would need to disappoint her as she was diverting her plan to see her, sufficing the call until she could visit with the woman called Jane, the sound healer.

"I need to postpone our meeting. I really meant to see you."
"When do you think you could be here?"
"I will think a day or two."
"I guess I will have to wait. You sure you can't come later?"
"I.. I meant, I'll try as soon as I can. I seem to have sprained my back."

A high-pitched screech, like a nail being dragged across a board set Michelle's ears pulling away from her cell.

"Michelle?"
"I'm here… just saying I…"

Screech.

196

"Hello?"

"The noise…". The screech continues as Julia yells, her voice drowned out. Michelle cringes, unable to keep the cellphone to her ear. The cell disconnects with a click.

Michelle closes her eyes. She opens them and sees shadows at the corner of her eyes. She turns and they vanish. She squeezes her eyes shut. The landline rings.

Michelle hears David enter the house and pick up the phone. She checks her watch, noting it's past six pm. She had slept for two hours."

"For you, hon."

"Julia?"

"No, this is Jane. The earliest I can see you is tomorrow afternoon."

"That's fine. I meant, that's really good."

"Sorry I couldn't get through your cell phone."

"Really? I wasn't on it the past few hours. I was asleep."

"Well, the message said it was not in service."

"I see. Glad you got a hold of me."

The landline rings again. The back door downstairs opens.

"Honey? You home?" David. Again.

"Of course. You just gave me the phone!"

David enters and hands the phone to Michelle. Michelle reels back, confused.

"You had already…". Michelle looks down at the phone in her hand. It was her cellphone.

Michelle places the cellphone on the bed, confused.

"Who… who is it?"

"It's someone about an appointment?"

197

"I… I…". She grabs the phone from David.

"Hello?"

"Yes, hi. This is Jane the sound healer. Is this Michelle Budke?"

"Yes. We just talked, didn't we?"

"No, I don't think so. I just got your message from the secretary."

"Oh." Michelle felt the onset of a dizzy spell.

"I have Tuesday, the day after tomorrow if that's open for you."

"I'll take it."

"See you then."

"I hope so."


Michelle put down the phone on the bed and stares at her cell phone. On the face, a text message had come through. She opens it.

"You think you can keep away from me?"

"Who is this?" Michelle types back.

"She can't help you."

"Who is this?!"

"LOL. She can't help you."

"Go away. You're not welcome." Michelle types.

"You know who I am?"

"Harry."

"Wrong!"

"I know who you are."

"Who am I?"

"In the name of Christ…"

"Go ahead. Name me."

"Go away."

"I know you, Michelle."


Michelle threw the cell phone on the carpet. The cell phone rang. She picks it up and another message comes in. She pauses, feeling her skin prickle. She clicks it on.

198

"I know you better than you know yourself, Michelle." A male voice said. It clicks.

## **Chapter Thirty Four**

I'm here for you, Michelle. I am here if you call me. I tried last night to warn you he would be coming. He whom I will not name is toying with you. And Clementine is still waiting for you to lead her to to the light as I am. We need you.

We need you. We won't and cannot allow ourselves to be stranded forever. We won't let you forget us.

Now he who is nameless is following you. He has been angered by your actions. Freeing those of us stranded in time and place is what we want, but he will try to stop you. On a planet we no longer belong because of our own trespass, is not of him. He wants us to languish in turmoil and sadness. He is despair. He is defeat. He doesn't know happiness. He wants us stuck.

He is the serpent you dreamt of; the bird that flies who is false. He is the man in the fedora hat. He is amplifying your dread and his need to destroy is strong. He has uncoiled himself from his despicable shape to shift into your space and home. He sits waiting to strike, posing first above your bed where you lay blissfully unaware of what lurks ahead.

Poor David loves you, but he is unable to protect you this time. But I can. I am ether. I am in the Neverland where the serpent sits. I can see him plain as day, plain as you, in this substance of things unseen by mortal man.

I am by his side, but not of him. I am the man who seeks salvation. I had no god and now must seek asylum within the rays of light no matter how weak for me. I need your inner light to rescue me and Clementine is waiting. She is attached to me because of my violent deed - and must repay her in a later life.

We need you.

He who does not repent and wants more is made of greed, hate, envy, pride and all things that negate life. He is serpent. He is outside your house, always in the shade of night. He seeks to destroy you. Please call on me. Please know the one named Alice in life is also here, but she is kind. She is like Clementine. She is not of me. Alice is kind. Alice can go anywhere where I cannot. Alice is attached to Harry even in death lest you break Harry's murderous cycle. He invades minds and makes them as corrupt as he.

He knows you. Please don't be afraid. But you must call on those who can protect you. You must. Before it's too late - he's coming after you.

We need you as much as you need us.

Michelle awakens. In the predawn light she spots past the solidity, comfort and seeming security of David, an apparition taking shape from the floor near their bathroom. Then, another. Two pillars of white smoke assume shape.

On the border of wakefulness and sleep, Michelle through human eyes see them skim the room and alight by her side. She turns her body to the right, away from the sleeping form of her husband; making eye contact with the weak light of the apparition - and the other - the gossamer threadlike substance that could be Clementine.

Michelle senses energy, though weak, speaking the language of desperation and benevolence. One a male, almost solid without a face; another, the feminine imprint of a young woman. Her energy feels lighter, almost bouncy. It is for sure Clementine. A murderer in life consumed by lust, his victim, still steeped in the naïveté and trust of youth, are wrapped in the inexorable embrace of karma.

202

This time Michelle's psyche, honed by time and spiritual experience, keenly as if with the finger of a lesser god, recognizes the entities as those who resided in her childhood closet. They had freed themselves in a step towards the light and taken residence in Michelle's house, offering the limit of protection a unfree spirit can bring.

203

## Chapter Thirty Five

## Michelle

Did you ever feel like your body wasn't your own? I had just celebrated my birthday a few months ago before I met Julia and Henry for the first time. I distinctly recall my children telling me I looked the day I did when I had my wedding photo with the exception of my slim waist and my thin arms that didn't need to be hidden as they do now. I felt the vigor of youth coarse through me then, my husband who was a few years older by three commenting on how he was now middle aged in his late fifties. When he turns sixty, I will be fifty seven.

Today, I felt old. I felt as if I'd bypassed my own mother, who at my age stood for several hours at her beauty shop and never had the issues I have now. It's obviously not our genes and hope Jess and Jake didn't have my misfortune.

The appointment was at three pm, but I found myself eager to seek relief from the pain which radiated from my back. Thus, I was at Jane's office right at two, a solid hour prior to the appointed time. While I waited, I attempted to screen out the pain which interrupted my concentration on a book by meditating on a single flower on a bud vase. A rose, just breaking open in the most delicate color of pink and mauve. I think they call it ashes or roses, a color that spoke to me and calmed me. It sat across from me on the cherry wood coffee table, the office now empty after the previous client.

Then, I saw it. Right in the stark incandescent lighting of fluted lampshades of the simple but well-appointed office, next to the brocade fabric settee in reds in yellows which matched the one I sat on, I saw it. Within a medium sized ceramic vase, Italianate and crystal, a face seems to stare back at me. Just a few feet from

205

the internal door of Jane's office. The vase was on top of a cherry wood bookcase which matched the coffee table.

I shut my eyes, perplexed, tossing the vision to my own broken internal compass, my own exhausted state, brought on by chronic pain. I rubbed my eyes, decided to exit the small waiting area for the bathroom located in the hall.

The bathroom had several stalls and washstands as Jane's office was housed in a medium-sized building downtown. I picked the third stall, entered and gingerly sat after feeling my back crack with the sudden movement to sit. Mindful now that I shouldn't attempt quick movements, I resolved to move slower, more conscious of the back pain which I did not want to exacerbate. Exiting, I proceeded to the closest washstand and attempted to reach for the soap dispenser when I detected movement behind me. I turned to find someone enter, the edge of their black skirt showing as the stall's door shut with a click.

I wash my hands, eyes to the mirror to check my makeup when behind me I saw movement within the stall. Someone was turning quickly or removing a dark article of clothing. A hat. A man in the women's toilet. Then I heard breathing, ragged and gasping as if someone was having difficulty catching their breath.

Then, a chuckle issued from the stall. It was incompatible with the previous breath. I found myself rooted to the floor, unable to move.

An unsettling feeling came over me like a wet towel on a winter night. I felt naked to something that was imminently near me. The bathroom turned cold, as if a thermostat had been shut off. The temperature plummeted in the room.

Quickly, I wipe my hands, feeling something exiting the stall behind me - slowly but intently watching my back. Finally, I dash headlong for the door, pulling it open.

206

I aim for the chair where I once sat and turned.  Just in time for the glass vase and visage I had seen glow an angry red.  There were eyes within the vase looking back at me aglow with hate.  I couldn't quite compute in my mind, but knew it was no longer a misperception, but it was real as the feeling in the bathroom.
The adjacent door suddenly opens and I stifle a scream.  A petite brunette woman in her forties smile a warmth that sent waves of comfort over me.

"Michelle Budke?"

It was Jane, the sound healer.

207

# Chapter Thirty Six

"Off the bat, I will tell you the limits of my intervention."
"I understand."
"My intention is to re-center you emotionally and try to promote spiritual equilibrium."
"That's what I want."
"However, the caveat is… if you've got a physical condition, your body will still scream to be rebalanced by some other way than me."
"Okay."
"The vibrations of healing inherent in sound frequencies aim to realign your chakras. You know what chakras are?"
"Energy centers in the etheric body. Our body."
"Yes, and you know there are seven chakras - seven energy centers from the top of your head to the base of your spine."
"Yes. The highest being the crown chakra on the forehead."
"Correct. These sounds will open the crown chakra and the one in your solar plexus."
"Okay. What can it do to protect me from these entities… the bad ones?"
"That's a separate intervention… one which demands you to do prior to entering an unholy place or one that may be inhabited by souls."
Michelle nods. "I'd like to learn that."
"It's simpler  than you may think, but it asks for faith, which is hard."
"I understand."
"Rituals are easy, but faith rides on the wings of belief."
"I believe."
"These entities will demand of you to enter the spaces of belief and beyond that, the sacredness of faith."

Jane stands, turns her back on Michelle and approaches a machine with several dials. The contraption is among several other pieces of period pottery, glass vases and brass bowls with wooden mallets placed on the side. Each bowl sat on an embroidered small pillow, tastefully decorating the sanctuary.

Michelle admired the bowls which were evidently made of brass and sone appeared adorned with etchings. Jane turns on a machine and turns.
"The bowls also harmonize our internal disquiet. It mutes the chatter of worry inherent in our three-dimensional brains."
Michelle nods, her interest piqued by the woman's discourse.
"The bowls are decorative but are very much part of my repertoire of meditation. Have you heard of them before?"
"No, they're new to me."
"We will try them at a later time. I will show you where to get them if you choose to get one for your use. There are several depending on size."
"Different sizes with different sounds?"
"Yes. But since this is our initial session, let's begin with the power of sound."
"I like music."
"That's good. Certain types of music touch our minds and hearts differently. You know that."
"Yes."
"First, I will ask you a series of questions…"

Outside the room, the vase sits with it's marbled glass reflecting the late afternoon sun. Something stirs within the design, coiling and uncoiling.

210

## Chapter Thirty Seven

Julia enters the kitchen, bright with touches of peach and yellow curtains that served as a backdrop to the large window over the sink. Although the kitchen is modestly furnished, outdated and small in size, Julia delighted in making the most of her center of activity as warm as she could manage. Under her arm, she produces a basket laden with fresh vegetables and flowers and lays them on the round small table that served as their breakfast area.

Today will be a different kind of day, she tells herself as she attempts to smooth out her hair, tied in a bun over her head. Sweat beads line her forehead as she leans over the table to place the broccoli heads on one side, the string beans, bell peppers and carrots on the other. Disappointment lines her face as she recalls the tirade over dinner last evening when Henry refused dinner and stormed out to get a drink at the local bar. Filled with worry, Julia had lost her appetite despite the dinner of shepherd's pie which she had prepared, something reminiscent of the days when they used to live in New England. The argument began as soon as he entered the kitchen, spotting the steaming dish she had prepared and indicated his distaste of lamb and peas, a former favorite.

The sun was out, its rays radiating on the outside barbecue and table for four, the prelude to summer which promises to be torridly hot. Julia plans on enlisting Henry to barbecue the beef ribs as he's prided himself in hosting barbecue parties a while back before the sinister events of the past months. She decided she'd invite him to help prepare the meal, the apron at ready, while she prepared the vegetables and would add them as a side dish - separate from the beef just in case he showed no interest in them. Stave off another argument, she hoped and thought the night air of the cooler evening would do them both a better state of mind. She couldn't surrender to the idea that it was something not of this world that was destroying their haven of peace, no matter how modest. Surely it was bad enough with the rising cost of living in New England that they had to give away half their furniture to move to a house old and much smaller in size than the one in Massachusetts.

As Julia washed the vegetables, chopped them and exited to the barbecue, she noted the absence of Henry's truck and recalled he was returning about five. For once, the television sets had been moved out of the rain and into the garage. That gave her a chance to move the bistro table and wrought iron chairs for four towards the deeper part of the shade of a large tree located at the front of the house. Away from the television and the garage. She could no longer tolerate the eerie feeling she received from the garage and the wooded area beyond it. Thankful she had prepared in advance, she proceeded to move the patio furniture and then the barbecue grill itself, albeit without a man's assistance, but the walking and exercise which gave her an opportunity to be away from Henry gave her the strength she needed.

Julia uncovers the barbecue, the plastic cover cracking with age. She reaches down to look for the utensils for the barbecue and finds none. She spots the garage behind the house and realizes they're in the garage, somewhere near Henry's tools. With trepidation, Julia trots across the grass, past the house and towards the open garage door and enters. She would be quick and grab them off the wall.

The cool air of the garage made Julia's arms prickle. She shook her tee shirt which had clung to her back with sweat. Off on a far wall past the television sets and wiring, hung the utensils lined on hooks. She grabs a large fork, another one for picking up the ribs and a third one, a spatula, and swiftly walks towards the door to exit.

That's when she heard it. The distinct beat of drums. Their rhythm made her edgy, almost breaking out in a cold sweat. It was not like her. It was coming from somewhere behind the garage. The woods.

213

Julia steps out into the sunshine and senses a change in the atmosphere. The sun had began its course down towards the shelter of the woods, interrupted suddenly by the massive stone fortress of the prison. It was suddenly dark and the silence deep. The birds which chirped and swooped down towards the picnic table in front were suddenly absent. The drums were more frantic, repetitive and insistent. There was an urgency to them now.

Quickly, Julia dashes to the front of the house, places the utensils on the side of the barbecue and turns the gas on to heat the grille. She surveys the area as she turns the knob, attempting to determine where the sounds were coming from.

In Jane's office, Michelle lies back, her feet up on the hassock. The sound healer watches as she shuts her eyes, her hands clasped and resting on her stomach. Jane turns up the volume and plays drumming music, akin to a beat of African drums. Michelle's eyes fly open and she searches the room.
"How are you feeling."
"I don't know. It's strange."
"In what way?" Tell me specifically.
"I feel like I can't concentrate. My toes are tingling."
Jane adjusts the knob on the machine and the drumming sound yields a different tone.
"How's this."
"Let me think on it… Better."
"From one to ten. Ten being it makes you jittery."
"Five. It's better than before."
Jane adjusts the knob again and turns another knob. The sound is deeper, lower in octave. Jane turns the dial to lower the volume.
"I like that."
"Great. We'll stay with that."
A gong. Soft and deep.
"I like that."

214

"That's a gong. Tibetan too. Be right back. Let that lull you to sleep."

Julia dashes for the front walk near the front path to the house, surveying if a neighbor was responsible for the drumming. A teen home from school practicing? She thought not, as the drumming sounded too good and too perfect in its unsettling way. She turns to return to the barbecue by the shade of the tree in front and spots the utensils scattered on the grass. Puzzled, she picks up the utensils, glancing around and turning in circles to see if Henry had tossed them and somehow arrived without her hearing him.

The drums were frantic now and drowning out the landscape. Julia looks at the street, noting the absence of cars, except for her red Toyota. She felt alone, yet not alone. She proceeds with the large fork in her right hand, surmising to use it as a weapon as she returns to the glass grille, the smoke coming now in tendrils. She opens it.

Smoke pours out of the grille. Julia takes a dish towel from the table and fans it around, dispelling the smoke, covering her nose. She coughs in reaction as she pulls away, the thick smoke barring her view of the grille. The smell of something like trash and something rotting assails her senses. Then she approaches as the drums from the wood raise in tone, rappelling her ears in a deafening crescendo. She could feel the drums shake the core of her being with everything vibrating around her, even the leaves and the tree itself that towered over the barbecue area she had created.
She spots the dials on the grille and reaches to turn them off, scolding herself for not checking the grille before turning it on. She peers into the grille, still smoldering.
The smoke disperses as she looks in:

A dead rat lies burnt on its side on the grille, eyes looking out, the fur smoking. The drums get louder as she gawks at the rat in disbelief. The animal's side was

215

open and rife with maggots. She screams, but her voice is covered by the sound of drums.

Michelle's eyes fly open. The drums thrummed through her chest and she sits bolt upright.
"Oh my Lord."
Jane dashes back to the room in alarm as the drums quake, drowning out any sound as it takes over, reaching a crescendo. She bolts for the dials on the machine, turning it down to no avail. Finally, Jane reaches behind the tall bookcase and reaches in for the electric plug. She pulls.

Silence.

"Something is happening." Michelle sits up in alarm. Her entire body shakes.
"I don't know what just happened! Everything was fine when I left."
"I must go."
"No, wait. You need to learn to ground yourself."
"I can't stay long. Something is telling me…"
"It won't take a minute, but believe me, you need to have a ritual of protection."
"Teach me now."

Julie bolts away from the grille, disgusted and terrified. Someone put that rat in there. The plastic cover was securely fastened on, safely shielding the interior from vermin. She surveys the area and her eyes lock on the tree line. A man, a deep shadow, cloaked it seemed, stood at the edge of the wood. It appears to be watching her. She couldn't see his eyes under the fedora hat, as if he had none.

Julia feels bile rise to her throat as the collective disgust of the dead rat and the sinister man confront her. She'd had enough. She dashes into the kitchen and vomits in the sink. Dry heaves follow as she looks up the kitchen window. The specter of the man had disappeared.

216

She bolts for the lock on the kitchen door, but sees Henry make his way around the side of the house, his truck now parked in front of the garage. He darts for the grille and grabs the large fork.

Julia watches Henry reach into the grille and fork the dead rat, still smoking. He darts to the side of the house, enters the kitchen and stands with the rat hanging off the fork.

"What is this? With one quick movement, he steps on the trash bin as the lid flies open and deposits the rat into the trash. The lid clangs shut.

"How did that get in there?! It was covered."
"You're asking me?" Henry's eyes exuded rage.
"I have to clean in."
"I'm not eating anything you grille."
"I was hoping you'd…"
"I'm not cooking or cleaning after you."

Henry dashes out, the back door screen slamming after him. Through the kitchen window she sees him dart towards the garage, make a sharp turn and follow the man in the shadows of the tree line. The man in the shadows turns his head towards Julia and red eyes leer back at her as if daring her to follow. He tips his hat. The man appeared solid, not just a vestige of a shadow as she had seen before.

Julia backs away and bolts for the front door. The drums reverberate throughout the house as she makes for her car parked at the curb. The drums beat, drowning out the car's motor as she turns the ignition.

217

## Chapter Thirty Eight

"Help. I need to get out of there."
"I can come now."
"No, no, no!  It's bad.  Really bad.  I just need someone to help me pack my things."
"We will say a prayer together.  I will see if I can try something else before you give up."

Julia visibly shivers as she wipes her eyes.  She takes in the large store, as if the antiques and books would bestow an answer, a remedy and a respite to the doom that had befallen her home and marriage.  She scanned the room, finally resting on one chair near her, a settee in period brocade from the seventeenth century.  She appeared to Michelle to be on the verge of a nervous breakdown.  Michelle observes the petite woman who at one time controlled and dominated the conversation with questions and suspicion.  The woman before her was merely a shadow of her former self, her tires deflated by her rocky life.

Michelle offers a tissue,  placing one arm around the woman in an attempt to console her.  It was half past six and passers by glance at the storefront window, some pause and some too harried on their way home.  Contrary to storekeepers who crave traffic into the store, Michelle hoped no one would enter for a while until she could better decide her next steps on behalf of Julia.

Michelle lists in her head the interventions which she had done and recommended: The prayers to the Celtic druids, the Indians who protected the forest behind the home and the Saint Michael prayer she faithfully recited prior to each visit.  It was followed by a referral to the local church and then another, each inhibiting the flow of evil in the home.  But then with sudden vengeance, the soul of Harry seemed

219

more entranced by Henry's personality and the shift became palpable to Michelle. It was as if the interventions from the local priest provoked the spirit, clearly marking it as a malevolent entity, refusing to let go.

Michelle surveys the store, searching for Uncle John who had disappeared to another area. Julia had entered disheveled and so distraught so he had wandered off to give the woman some measure of privacy with Michelle. Michelle had quickly offered the woman a seat by the register, her spot inside the counter abandoned for the moment.

"Come. Come to the kitchen and have something to eat while I finish my shift."
"I can't. I lost my appetite all together."
Michelle paused and finally spotted her uncle milling about, dusting and straightening one of the displays of jewelry. They make eye contact and he nods, walking to a nearby display case by the front entrance. He reaches into the case, moving things in order while watching for visitors.
"Stay here. Don't go anywhere. I'll be right back."

Michelle dashes to the kitchen area, sensing the presence of someone watching there. She enters and smells perfume, now becoming more familiar. She turns on the cat balls and the EVP. They light up and then the balls roll towards her. Alice is back.

"Alice."
The cat balls go green.
"Julia is here. Is Harry back?"
The EVP goes wild.
"Come. Come with me to Julia's house."
The cat balls light green. Yes.

Michelle grabs a thin vessel in a glass container, the one end with a stopper. She hold it up to the light of the kitchen and the vessel is filled with salt. A tube larger

220

than a test tube. She approaches the counter where medals were strewn, each wrapped in plastic. They appear to have just been purchased. She grabs a handful and places them in her left pocket, placing the other vessel in her right.

Eyes shut, Michelle murmurs the Our Father. Visions appear as she opens her eyes. Go. I will tell you what is happening there, she hears in a whisper in her etheric mind. Then, a flash in her mind's eye of the day at the school playground when a lady who arrives with a brightness came to reassure her. A warmth fills her being, but the vision is cut short. She feels the onrush of dread, as if something was coming her way she couldn't prevent.

Julia sits, surveying the articles for sale around her. She turns as she hears the soft pad of feet. It was Michelle, her handbag around one shoulder and another holding a duffel bag.

"Let's go in my car. Is there anyone you can stay with just in case it gets late?"
Julia stands, a light in her eyes. "Oh, I hope you can fix what is happening."
"I have to get a sense of the place again. Whatever it is keeps returning with a vengeance."
"I can call my sister in the next town and stay with her if all else fails."
"I strongly feel it's worth another try."
Julia slowly nods, eyeing something by Michelle's feet. Michelle looks down and sees a cat ball, the green light on.
"It rolled towards you."
"Yes."
"This is all too strange for me."
"I understand."

Julia sits on the passenger side of Michelle's late model Jeep, as she fastens her seatbelt. "Before we go we're going to pay a quick visit to Jane, my sound healer. I was just there when things were unraveling this afternoon at your house. I sensed the drums and they were going wild in Jane's office."

221

Julia stared back, dumbfounded.

"You... you heard the drums going off in my property? Outside?"

"Not literally with my ears. I sensed them. However, I did awaken from my meditation to the drums in the office going up and getting loud. Getting discordant."

"Are you telling me the drums I heard weren't my imagination?"

"The drums you heard exist only for you and brought on by Harry, I feel. You were being attacked psychically and I sensed it with my abilities."

Julia slowly nods, enrapt. Her internal critic still intact.

"I meant, Alice's old nemesis and late husband who was executed for what he did to her may be the root cause for Henry's change in his personality. Harry sensed some kind of kinship with Henry. So Harry has returned to the place he has been frequenting in life as he awaited his execution: The wood behind your property and the field beyond. He's literally trying to drum you out of Henry's existence - meant maybe to get you anxious and scared and destroy Henry, the person you know."

"Well, if this is so, this Harry is succeeding."

"Evil people destroy. In death, they are stranded to haunt and seek to destroy souls - and of course latch on to living people who signal by their own vibration their misery and anger."

"So... this Alice maybe is trying to save Henry or my marriage."

"Yes. Alice was a victim in life of an evil person. Good ghosts like Alice stay for a reason. Not just because they fancy attaching themselves to an antique. Once their mission has been identified, they let go of the object. In this case, a teapot."

Michelle recalls the teapot and how paranormal team member Nancy finally had a chance to purchase the beautiful and elegant object. Nancy, a gentle and kind woman, was overjoyed.

Michelle turns the wheel and reaches a four-way stop. She turns in her seat to observe a puzzled Julia, still troubled, but in disbelief.

"Why me?"

222

Michelle allowed the question to linger, mulling over a sound explanation that may be more plausible than another. She didn't want to appear as a toter or crystal balls, peddling her psychic wares. There were many charlatans out there and she gave her services and time for free, unlike some who sought payment.

"You're now pregnant as Alice was when he chose to murder her. You are inhabiting an area that catalyzed an evil man who is seeking to repeat his murderous act. He is doomed to repeat in death what he had done in life as he has no remorse."
"Oh, God."
"Your life path mirrors Alice's life… let's hope you are saved and Henry too."
"Please. This is highly strange. I'm terrified if this is true, but there's no explanation."
"As I said before, I was in a sound healing session when I intuited through the drums that you were in distress. My drums replied to your anxiety tenfold as I lay there, to signal to me your situation."
"This Alice - she has contacted you? His late wife?"
"She has been. She is trying to help us not repeat history by trying to save you. Break the cycle."
"Through you."
Michelle nods as she drives towards the southern end of Leavenworth. The prison looms ahead as Michelle steers the vehicle past the street that led to the prison on the west side.

"Henry might be home."
"He may. I will see if Jane is available to validate what I think may be happening, but I must visit to be sure. She lives near her practice."
"Validate?"
"I meant, validate what I think might have happened as a result of my visit to the prison to verify the identity of the entity infesting your house through Henry."
"Henry has become very strange. I'm afraid of what he might do."
"First, we may have to remove a curse."

"A curse?"

"A curse Harry might have placed on your property. I don't know yet."

Julia's eyes take on a new light, like a lightbulb going off. "There's definitely a man in a cloak of some type on the property. Red eyes. I saw him staring at me and Henry went with him."

Michelle feels a new dread, even a sense of despair enter her psyche.

"I hope it's not too late."

"If it is, what do I do?"

224

225

## __Chapter Thirty Nine__

Jane exits a house with a well-tended garden, resplendent in pink and purple flowers in a sea of green. As Michelle leads her back to the car, Julia steps out and Michelle introduces Jane. Julia notices the woman is carrying a drum, like those she'd seen in movies used by American Indians. A medal, similar to those she sees sold at church shops, is around the woman's neck, glinting against the streetlights. She also had a rosary wrapped around her hand.
Jane enters the back seat of Michelle's Jeep and Julia smells the distinct scent of Jasmine and something very clean. She sniffs.
"It's sage." Jane comments, as if reading Julia's thoughts.
Julia turns to the back seat and smiles, comforted. The woman had penetrating eyes.

Michelle guns the jeep towards the downtown area.
"Let's pray together and dine. Okay?" Jane suggests.
"Hopefully the diner isn't crowded. I'd like to get a table with some privacy to discuss…"
"Oh, I'm starved I can have an entire side of beef." Julia exclaims.
Michelle smiles at the rearview. "Glad your appetite has returned."

The sounds of car doors shutting shatters the silence as Michelle exits the car with Jane and Julia. It was ten p.m. by the time they left the diner. Behind her, Julia trails with Jane following a few paces behind. Michelle pauses, surveying the front of Julia's home from the front lawn. The house was completely dark, the windows devoid of light and life.

"I don't hear the television. He doesn't look like he's home." Julia whispers, stating the obvious. "But he could be sitting and waiting for me."

226

Michelle raises one hand to signal the women to stop. She trots ahead, her sneakers squeaking in the dampness of the thick grass. To her right, she passes the open grille, now empty of the dead rat that frightened Julia hours ago. A table and chairs in wood are set up nearby, in anticipation of a picnic. The feel of the picnic table and grille, merry during the day now served to hint at an abandoned spot.

The kitchen door, the screen partially ajar from Henry's hasty exit to the woods, yawed against the night, the door almost new, glinting its silver brackets in silence. The side of the house with its windows shut didn't evince anyone looking out. Michelle digs in her pockets, searching for her rosary. She realizes in their haste to get seated they had forgotten to pray.

The garage peers behind the house, several yards away. Past it, the tree line stood, as if forbidding Michelle to enter its depths. A sense of unease besets her as she walks forward, the sound of crickets and frogs from the swampy field beyond the right of the house hailing the night.

Halfway to the garage, Michelle pauses to take in her impressions. Elementals peer back at Michelle from the wood: Dwarves, gnomes, American Indians who protected the integrity of the land. Harmless guardians of nature, halted in their tracks by man's footprint, willing to intervene should one destroy the fertile ground and the diversity of creatures they inhabit. They wait as if they knew what had transpired hours ago in the light of day, now in anticipation of the next. Michelle is here and she is welcome, she senses as a guardian of nature in her own right. She couldn't see where the prison's tall and solid walls of cement began, but she knew it was there: The stark darkness of the wood was a combination of the understory, the sheltering trees and the stars overhead blocked by the fortress beyond.

Suddenly, something was coming through the trees. Crickets and frogs, owls and nocturnal animals pause in pregnant wait. A seamless void exits from the depths of wood, penetrating darkness as if a shape attempts to form and force the tree branches to break. Suddenly, a deep pregnant pause of silence descends on the

227

area as if the creatures of the forest and field had held their breath. It was as if no one else in the neighborhood lived just yards away. No traffic passed and no children in sight.

Michelle continues to dig in her jeans pocket for the rosary.

A branch cracks. Michelle braces for what seems to be something rolling towards her without pause. She listens with her etheric ear and unconsciously adjusts her glasses. She squints to look into the depths of the trees ahead. Whatever it was, was getting closer. She turns to check on the women behind her and raises her hand, staying them from going further. Julia cowers, backing away towards the curb as if ready to run as Jane gently places a hand on the woman's shoulder.

A breath. Michelle's skin prickles as something beckons her, whispering something unintelligible in her left ear. Unconsciously, she turns her head, straining her eyes to see. A flash of light and she turns to find Julia holding a small penlight, shining it through the trees. Something swiftly hides behind a large tree in reply, as if blinded.

"Henry! Is that you?"
Michelle's voice travels and then echoes back by the walls of the prison.

The penlight weakens and blinks out. Michelle hears Julia's hand clicking away in an effort to turn the flashlight back on. The woman turns away and bolts for the curb of the street.

Suddenly, a darkness surrounds Michelle, shadows tall and leaning towards her with red eyes confront her in a circle. The grass reaches up to her as if to swallow her. Michelle sinks to her knees as she finally finds her rosary, revealing it. The rosary breaks in a string, scattering the beads all over the ground.

228

In vain, Michelle reaches for the crucifix, intoning a prayer that she seems to have forgotten. She grasps for the words to no avail. She senses her throat closing in. It wasn't Alice. It wouldn't be. She strains to remember the face of Mary Michelle, who said she'd be wherever she was, so long ago. She remembers the holiness of the moment.

A viselike grip surrounds Michelle's throat, ratcheting shooting pains down her back as she struggles to reach up and sit up. Jane dashes towards her, tripping on something invisible. Michelle sees the woman as if she's miles away as the woman struggles to get up, yelling something she couldn't hear. At the edge of her vision, much further away, Julia. She is running towards her, but stops in disbelief at something behind Michelle she couldn't see.

Michelle's vision narrows as she realizes another presence more powerful than Alice hovering near her. It was behind her. She turns and turns in a circle, attempting to confront the intruder as she glimpses there and again a deep darkness behind her, pushing the limits of her faith and seeking to dispel her grounded attitude with doubt.

A sense of foreboding grips her body. The thought that comes next is Harry. Harry in Henry. Henry in Harry. A man seems to be standing just behind her within the limits of her vision to the left. The same man whose voice mimicked David's, telling her there was a call on the phone. Then the eerie and terrifying text message that came through in the privacy of her own home, her own sacred space.

He is right behind her to her left.
Her back screams as Michelle keeps turning in a circle, attempting to see what appears to be the edge of a cloak… dark and carrying with it the scent of decay and something ancient and infernal. It dawns on Michelle it is the scent of death.

Like quicksand, finally her knees sink into the grass, swallowing her. Michelle's vision narrows and she hears a man's laughter as she passes out.

229

## Part Three:

### Attack

231

232

# **Chapter Forty**

## **Forgiveness**

Lights, a movement, more lights from above. A doctor's face. Her mother, worry lines and eyes. A man sits at her right, hands clasped around his knees. He looks awfully familiar and she senses love.
David.
David is wearing jeans, not his normal suit. It must be Saturday. What was yesterday?
She attempts to turn her head to the left and the pain shoots up her head from her spine and neck. She can't turn left.
"It's dad, Michelle. Don't try to turn your head."
A hand, masculine, calloused and aged, grasps her left hand. She attempts to look down and an IV is bandaged to a vein in her hand.
"Keep looking forward, dear." The sound of her mother's voice reassures her.
Glasses. Someone places glasses back on her face.
"You really disengaged your back, somehow. Jane told us you kept turning to your left as if you wanted to twist your entire body." David trying to explain as David would.

Charlene adjusts Michelle's glasses, smiling a worried smile as she leans back to assess Michelle. The world comes back to focus. Charlene, her dear mother, all hair now silver in a thick bun with curly q's framing her face.
Jessica sits at the foot of bed, staring at something. A chart. She sees her face in her own daughter, once when she was just a teen. The same face, now lined with worry like her mother.
"Dad, she needs more water." Jake. Jake's youthful voice, higher than usual. He is anxious.
A glass with a plastic straw and water. She sips.

233

Then, exhaustion overtakes her. Michelle closes her eyes, comforted by her family around her. Am I dying? What happened to me? Then, she remembers forgetting to pray and forgetting a prayer while she groped for her faith in the presence of terror. She recalls the rosary beads scattering as she reached for the crucifix that was mercilessly snatched from her hand.

She senses movement, then her body slumps as if riven with despair. She had forgotten to protect herself and the women behind her.

A beeper rings somewhere beyond and she senses a shift.

She's in a room. Her childhood bedroom.

The closet opens slowly. Gently.

Michelle looks down at her own feet. The feet of a six-year-old child. Her feet. Another foot steps near her. A foot not much larger than hers. Another child. Lace. The edges of the child's nightgown next to her. Her own was in blues and pinks.

The scent of lily of the valley fills the room.

She looks up.

The closet is completely open. Michelle gasps, astonished that the object of her childhood dread is back.

Michelle hears the voice of one so familiar and so far away. "Michelle."

"Mary Michelle, is that you?"

"Yes. I'm here."

"I missed you."

"I missed you too, Michelle."

"You never grew up, Mary Michelle."

"But you did. You must pray now and break the cycle."

"Cycle?"

"The cycle of karma."

"How?"

234

"You must do this. This will help you for the next one. The next one is real evil."

A man exits without a face from the closet.
"Who are you? You're the one who's real evil?"
"No, he is the one who begged for you to save him. He who seeks forgiveness."
Mary Michelle responds. "From your childhood."
"He scared me, Mary Michelle!"
"No, you can handle it now. You're older."
"I no longer have to run to Mom and Dad?"
"Not anymore. You have the Light now."

"Free me please so I may help you against the evil one." The phantom from the closet had a voice though he remained faceless.
Michelle turns to Mary Michelle. She nods. Michelle wonders why her neck doesn't hurt when she turns. She can turn, she discovers with glee.

Freed from pain, Michelle turns to her left, astonished to find the phantom there. A man. Just another spirit. She lays a hand on the man's shoulder, who stood in wait. He smiles in anticipation, radiating an inner light that appears to be growing from her touch.
A girl, sixteen years young, wearing slippers and a blue sleeveless dress reveals herself. "You hurt me greatly. You destroyed my life, but I now can forgive you." The girl says, her voice like water, as she addresses the faceless man. "I am breaking the cycle."

The girl reaches her hand out, slim and with vigor towards the man. "Michelle has amplified my energy of courage to forgive."
The teen reaches for the faceless man's shoulder. "I forgive you."
In reaction, the man screams and cries, his tears melting his face. He appears to be in agony, his apparition splitting in two from head to toe and then reassembling, seeking redefinition.

235

His body twists, he gasps, then his face softens as if beckoned by something unseen.

Suddenly, he stops. "Please forgive me."

For the first time, Michelle sees his brilliant blue eyes as he looks up at the ceiling at something unseen, even to Michelle. His face shines in ecstasy, an inner light awed at something above them:
"Please, forgive me. I do not want to do anything ever again as I did to Clementine. Ever."

A hole opens and they collectively look up. A radiant blue light slices through the ceiling, widening the hole. A light emits and shines on the man, his blue eyes wide with joy and awe.
"I've been forgiven... been forgiven... been forgiven..."
Michelle can now see features on the man, his light cheeks, his arms, his hair, reddish and wild. He brims with youth as in life.
He turns with a warmth and a smile to Michelle. "Go." Michelle hears herself say. "Clementine has forgiven you and God of course has."
"We are free." Clementine intones in a chant. "We are free."
"I am free. I am no longer afraid." The man said with joy radiant on his face.
"I'm so happy. I will come back and help you." The man said, tears of joy in his eyes.

Then, in a flash he was gone, followed by the girl in blue, her brown eyes radiating. "I can live again." Clementine said. "His name was Paul in life. A lustful man. I forgive him... I forgive him... I forgive him..."

In a flash, sparkles flew to the halo of light, disappearing into the ceiling. Clementine has moved on.

"The cycle of karma had been broken." Said Mary Michelle.

236

Michelle moves towards the halo and turns to Mary Michelle. "Where will you go now?"

"I am following you. Wherever you are, I am too." Mary Michelle ascends to the halo in the ceiling, reaching down with both hands with love and benediction.


"Wake up, Michelle. Julia is waiting for you."

Michelle awakens.

"Oh, thank God. The doctor's here, honey." Charlene's face, soothed by Michelle's wakefulness, stands in expectation. Michelle feels refreshed, as if from a dream.

"I have to go, Mom. Julia needs me."

"The doctor needs to talk to you and let you know what is happening."

"What's the matter, Mom? Are you all right? You're crying."

"No, I am fine. I'm glad you're back."

"I saw Mary Michelle."

"There's a problem with your spine, honey."

"Again?"

"Yes."

"But it already fixed when I was thirty-nine. It shouldn't be this way…"

Charlene touches her daughter's cheeks looking into her eyes. " But it is. Why, we don't know. So let's take care of you first. Then everything else will follow."

237

238

## **<u>Chapter Forty One</u>**

"The discs in your back, particularly those in your neck are deteriorating."

"How could that be? I meant, it's my son who plays golf and he's fine. He's got scoliosis - it's he we should worry about."

The silver-rimmed glasses of the doctor, stared back at Michelle. She could smell his cologne under his lab coat. The stool squeaks under his as he maneuvers his way towards the x-ray pinned to a lighted display.

"You're now in your fifties, correct?"

"Yes. Eighteen years ago I had a spine procedure. I had to get it to correct the discs on my back."

The doctor glances at David, who appeared as perplexed.

"Sorry to say. The procedure you had needs to be remediated. We need to refer you to a surgeon to fix it or you won't be able to walk."

"That's probably why you fainted. You were in so much pain, weren't you?" David asks.

"I am still. I can't believe the pins aren't holding."

"I will refer you if you like, but it has to been sooner than later."

"How long can I put it off?"

"Honey, you can't." David appeared alarmed.

"No, you can't delay. It's crucial to get it addressed." The doctor's tone betrayed his deep concern.

"But why is it deteriorating? My diet?"

"I have no explanation why."

"Was this suppose to happen eventually? "

The doctor shook his head. "No, not for a while. These pins are good for at least twenty five years."

"It's only been eighteen years since I had the procedure."

"For some odd reason, the discs are deteriorating."

"Is this unusual?"

239

"Yes. Very."

"So, the procedure given to me long ago wasn't as good as we thought."

The doctor pauses, deep in thought. He struggles to get up from the stool, his posture conveying his own perplexity.

"No, the way your discs appear here?"

"Yes?"

"It looks like you were strangled and assaulted with such force as to make them that way."

David observes Michelle as she realizes with gnawing dread the events leading up to the pains in her back.

"Did you fall?" The doctor prods.

"No."

"Anyone assault you, mug you, have some type of altercation?" The doctor glanced at David, with growing suspicion.

"No, not David. No, he won't ever do that." Michelle lovingly glances at her husband, clutching his hand.

"This type of deterioration is usually seen when something mechanical is forcing you not to turn your head. Something twisting you with great force."

"Fighting with me?"

"Fighting for you not to do something. Like turn your head."

"I was trying to turn my head before I fainted."

"To do what if I may ask?"

"To see something coming up behind me."

"You were driving?"

"No. I was outside. On a lawn."

"I guess whoever it was didn't want you to turn and for you to see."

"I see."

"So you were not inside a car and driving perhaps?"

"No. I was outside."

"What were you doing outside?"

"I was trying to see who had approached from behind me."

"Who or what hit you with such force that your discs were dislocated and injured to this extent?"

241

242

# **Chapter Forty Two**

## **The Visitor**

There's only two things that could repel me, and you did neither one. IF you're going to play this game, play it well, Michelle. I would've thought that you'd be smarter, having had some time with that woman who heals with vibrations and learning how to deal with your gifts. Your senses, after all, is not up to snuff I would have to say, since you don't know what you're dealing with, playing with, messing with.

That was your first lesson in hastiness. What's the saying these days? Eat, pray, love? Well, I won't tell you what part you missed. That's the same part that Henry always misses. He's no challenge to us here in the fourth. He's just a toy to use to scare his wife. His poor wife who was too proud to say she could've prayed. She thought she could control everything. Well, not me and not Henry.

Second thing that repels me, I won't even mention to you. It's the same thing over and over. You investigators and mediums are so hell-bent, ha ha. Hell-bent to fix things as if there was a time limit here. We don't adhere to the time limit. There's no time limit in the fourth or fifth, or higher. We are, as your boy Paul of the closet who is now free to roam, has said.

We are timeless. You know what that means? We never tire of toying with you, with people like you, with people who think they're tough and prepared to play games with us. Oh no.

Are you ready for what my other repellent is? Like superman, we are repelled by Kryptonite. Ha ha. A joke. No, young lady. Not quite. However, like Kryptonite is to superman, your faith is our Kryptonite.

243

Faith. Okay, I mentioned it even though I told you I wouldn't.

Faith. That word that's so easy to say, but hard to do. You see, most of the world in the third dimension lacks faith. What do we do when we see no one we know? We dig in, dive in and destroy. We just simply love doing that. We toy with them, spin them around and around and around until they break. But see, there is someone stronger than you that we do know. AND we are afraid of Him. You too, if you're depraved like us, should be afraid of Him.

Paul was afraid of Him. Paul knew he needed you to be kind to him and encourage him, that lustful one, to go to the Light. Paul wanted to be sure if he emerged out of that closet he wouldn't be sent to eternal Hell by Him. You bitch. You had to save Paul. He could've joined us here and toy with more women. But you... you had to be nice. Stop it. Stop being nice.

Then there's Henry.

Henry is a fun one. Not much of a challenge in my estimation. He sits all day playing with his toys, his tools and boy, his hate radiates and attracts me. Yeah. In life I hated my wife. You know her very well by now. Did you really think she can help you? I know Alice like the back of my etheric hand: The hand in life that slapped her, that stupid bitch. I'm going to do to Julia what I did to Alice. I got nothing to lose. I was in jail and guess what? I'm in hell jail now, baby.

You try and stop me. I'll break your back before you do.

There's something else that comes to mind that tires me, puts me out and drains me. That third thing that drains me. That I'll never tell anyone including you. It would mean you'd have to be really good. Truly good. When you become that good, that makes you a challenge for us here that like to corrupt the incorruptible. I dare you to put that into practice.

I dare you, Michelle.

245

246

## **Chapter Forty Three**

Michelle pulls and tugs at the duffel bag, taking it out of the closet. It was not as heavy as she thought and didn't aggravate the pain in her neck. A pain in the neck, she thought. A pun on the case involving Julia; that stubborn entity that won't let go of Henry and has now become a monstrosity of a case.

Michelle inspects the contents of the bag which she had left in her car when she arrived at Julia's house. David had taken it out after the chaos that ensued at Julia's property, resulting in an emergency room visit. During the overnight stay, David checked the bag and found her vials of holy water under the drum, stowed in a compartment for safe-keeping. The medals, purchased from the church's shop, were blessed from the Lourdes cathedral in France. She recalls how they could've helped and perhaps prevented the entity which attacked her behind Julia and Henry's house. But then, as Michelle scrolled through her memories of the past visits in the haunted locations, she felt it was an earlier event where there may have been an entity that followed her out: The Selby house, the antiques shop - or the house where the slaves were abandoned to die? Or even as far back as the entity in the closet where Mary Michelle came to the rescue? Not that. They both crossed over and broke the cycle of Karma, those two.

Michelle scrolls through her memories, the pain in her back radiating in peaks and volleys like steel hitting her again and again. Like some force twisting her against her will to look behind her, as the doctor said. Who was watching her out there?

Then, it came with a vengeance and the overpowering scent of verbena: The prison. Her thoughts flooded back to the afternoon and evening when she and her daughter entered the prison with a group - and the cell in the 'dungeon'. Michelle suddenly sits, overpowered by a memory and the scent that heralded the entrance of Alice:

247

The tour. The tour she took with Jessica at their request with Ken LaMaster, the author and famous historian as docent. It was in the prison's 'dungeon' where she had first successfully liberated a soul or two, one who was bludgeoned and another prisoner afraid to go to the light.

Someone, a third entity, was present and watching her. It had to be the soul of the Nazi, the Aryan prisoner who had killed his fellow prisoner, the man's blood still cascading through the cracks of the cement floor in her mind's eye. The bludgeoned man, liberated, his soul flying through the ceiling in sparkles was witnessed by Michelle, but also by a dark entity who didn't want anyone to ascend. Perhaps the same one who clawed at her back and tried to push her down the stairs.

She recalls the sense of victory, of celebration and a sudden lightness that suffused the prison cell with light. She had ignited the rage of the dark entity in that small cell by liberating souls from the prison. A lesser spirit.

He must have followed her out. That night, she sensed a presence in the house, standing in the shadows and eventually, in her own bedroom. David, exhausted and sleepy, lay beside her unaware of the unseen that transpired hours before - her sense of victory soaring to a sense of spiritual uplifting that was detected by lesser spirits. That's when she first felt the pains that scaled her back. It had began with the scratches, the clawing while still at the prison.

David had cautioned Michelle with trepidation not to bring "anything" home from her visits to Julia's house after hearing about Henry and the garage. Michelle knew well his fears which became more alarming when the doctor explained the deterioration in the discs of her back, brought on by a 'strange force', according to the kind doctor. David's fears escalated after having heard what she had done, visiting the house behind the penitentiary where Julia's encounters had ratcheted, bringing on unexplained behaviors in Julia's spouse, Henry.

248

Michelle explains to David over dinner what she felt she could do and in her haste had not allowed herself the plenitude of protection that Jane had so strongly recommended. While they had dined, concerned about Julia, she scolded herself afterwards for her hastiness and perhaps placing at risk not just herself but Jane and Julia. As she sits over dinner that night with her husband who doted on her, she apologized for placing him in a state of worry.

Michelle would and from thereon master the methods of all paranormal investigators, mediums and exorcists when entering a possibly infested site: She would engage in protective steps prior to entering and close the investigation with prayers of protection. She knew better. She had just recently invested in all the holy objects that David found in the duffel bag. There was no excuse, Michelle scolded herself again and again, for the lack of foresight and the hasty entrance into a penitentiary and a property that she knew beforehand could carry menace and misfortune back to her home.

Michelle reluctantly stood from the dining table as David quietly filled the dishwasher with the night's flatware and dishes. She turns and finds David's face inches from her in a visage of forgiveness and worry. He reaches for her and kisses her.
"Before anything, we must make that appointment."
"I know. I meant to call this morning."
"Please take a break from this and refer it to someone else."
"I can't. If the church does it, it just amplifies whatever is in there. It takes too much red tape, too many months of proving and the priest - is exhausted. He's alone and needs help. Clergy are leaving the vocation like crazy."
"What else, then, is left to do?"
"I don't know. But you're right. I have to go through with the operation first. I must think  through things with a clear mind."
"You must. These cases are dangerous, it seems. You can't see…"
"I can to an extent. I try, but I must protect and pray before I get to the site."

249

250

## **Chapter Forty Four**

## **The Hospital**

There is a girl. She enters my hospital room in the garb of a patient, like me. Open gown in the back, closed in front. She is always walking in and then she looks at me with such soulful eyes, like she's tired, in despair and helpless. I say hi or hello and she just walks away like she didn't hear me. She usually comes in after the change of shifts at eleven in the evening. It's dark in the hall by then and I had just received my next dose of demerol and the water in my jug is fresh for the night. I thought I was dreaming. I meant, I am in a recovery wing and anything is possible when you're drugged.

I see her as I fitfully dose with the television on mute so that my roommate wouldn't awaken. My roommate, an older woman in her sixties, had slipped in the tub and hurt her pelvis. I made a mistake of mentioning the girl to her, asking her one day if she knew why a young girl, perhaps a patient in another ward would visit us. I meant, I thought she was her daughter or relative or something.

The older woman had looked back at me and looked puzzled. Who? When?

No idea. I thought maybe someone was coming to see you in the next ward. To stop in and check on how you were doing. I don't know her. She doesn't answer when I say hi.

When does she come? How old? A kid? A teenager?

Around the change of shifts at night. You know. When the nurses chat about us and changing our dressings, giving us more of the same meds. A girl of about twelve, maybe.

251

I have a son, not a daughter. His wife is pregnant, but no other kids. What does she look like?

Good question. She's got long dark hair, tied in a pony tail. She just seemed sad all the time like she's looking for someone.

Well she won't find anyone she knows here. Just us older women with something broken. I got to get back to my show. Okay, I say, and try go back to my book, but I'm too sleepy. She unmutes her TV and I reach for the clicker, channel surfing. In another hour, the physical therapist walks in, her sneakers immaculately white like it was new.

The next night, I saw a young man peer in with a look of surprise. I looked right back at him and said hello as I normally do. Nosy, I thought. He seemed like he heard my thoughts and looked annoyed, even shocked that I saw him peek. Yeah, you must have died, I thought. You're surprised that I can see you. I know. I sound like the movie where the kid tells Bruce Willis, "I see dead people."

The next night, the girl was back promptly at eleven. I put two and two and realize, yes she's dead too. But I had to test it.
Emma, I said. Emma, she's back. Look.
Emma stirred from reading her magazine and looked up at the door. She looks back at me like I was losing a few cards in my deck. What? Did I miss her again?

She's right there. Hey, there. Who are you? Are you lost?

Emma chuffed and turned back to her book. I don't see who you're talking to. You're talking too much of that stuff that makes you high. Then I knew. The girl was a...

252

I went to sleep. It had been weeks. Before you know it, I was up and dressed. I was going home. That afternoon, I found out a young girl had passed down the hall from her injuries sustained in a car accident. I saw her face on the paper. It was the same girl, not yet thirteen, looking back at me with soulful eyes. She didn't know she was dead.

As David wheeled me out of the ward, unable to move with the brace and stitches in my back, I scanned with my eyes. Down an adjacent hallway, dim even during the day, stood the young man who peered into my room. He stood, waving at me, as if to say goodbye. I waved back. He turned and walked away and vanished.

I still had my gift though I was drugged. I could still 'see' even in the midst of haziness that enveloped me in my stay.

I must look crazy.

253

254

# **<u>Chapter Forty Five</u>**

Drums. I heard drums. I don't know why Jane would be here. Jane, is that you drumming? I can't see. I hear you. I need to be somewhere, but I can't seem to move. Then, I heard flapping of wings. Something swiped my forehead, like a bird's wing. That can't be right. I'm not outside. The last time I was outside…

I cough. I try to sit up. I faintly move my arms, pinwheeling them as I try to rest my elbows on the bed, trying to get up.

"Michelle. Let me help you, honey."
David. David is near me. On our own bed.
"I can't move."
"It's all right. You're in a brace, remember?"
Oh, my gosh. Please. When will it come off?"
"Soon. Please let me help."
David moves and I am pushed up. I look around the dim light of morning and strain to turn and see my husband. A smile escapes from his eyes, traveling down to his lips. The man I married, the father of my children, is smiling down at me. I felt fat, huge, ugly and old.
"No, you're not. You'll be well soon and no pain will bother you again."
I must've said it out loud.
"You're feeling bad right now so you feel old. It's the brace. It will come off."
"Okay. I need to move to the edge of the bed."
David moves me and I swing my feet heavily to the side of the bed. I sit up with his assistance. I felt my bladder move me faster, faster than I'm suppose to move.

"I'll make coffee downstairs. Jane called and asked about you. The team too… Nancy, Cheryl, you know… Rich and Brenda."
"Yes, the nurse said I had visitors, but I was asleep so they told them."

255

"Heard anything from Julia?"
"She's moved to her sister's until the house can be sold, according to Jane."
"Oh. I feel sorry I can't do anything for her right now."
"She's out of harm's way."
"I'm so relieved, but not for the next owner of that house."

Suddenly, my head swims as I try to remove my nightgown, reaching for the bathtub's edge. I detect movement behind me. I felt a comforting touch. The scent of verbena.
That would be Alice.

"Alice?" I search for the cat balls which lie around the house, always with batteries charged. None were in the bedroom. "Crap. David?"
I feel movement, footsteps downstairs. He must be preparing coffee.
"David, can you get the cat balls down there and bring them up, please?"
Did Alice follow me from the antique store? I steadied myself, wondering what the scent meant. What compelled her to attach herself to me? Julia's case. Yup. Did she follow me home?
"David?"
Silence.
"David?"

I shrug on my sweats, hampered by the brace on my back. The pain from the injury now gone, but replaced by the stitches which marked the recency of my major operation. As I slowly move to dress myself, I realized I had a physical therapy appointment coming up. I had to check the calendar on the refrigerator for the time, so decided to go downstairs, albeit slower than usual. It was taking me longer to shower. Although it was now safe to wet my stitches with the water coursing through me, it was tough negotiating myself around the house with a brace that restricted my movements.

256

I dry myself the best I could, then trudged out to dress, opening the dresser. The clock face stared back at me and there it was: It was six in the evening. What happened to the time? I was just getting up?

"David?" Something was shuffling downstairs.
I felt myself grow cold and reached for my clothes, struggling to dress. What happened with the time? I turn slowly to look out the bedroom window, turning with care and slowly to check the light outside. That's when I realize it's night. I had lost an entire day.

257

258

# **Chapter Forty Six**

Verbena fills the air. "Alice. Are you here?"

I found myself whispering to no one. David wasn't home. Where was he? Did I fall asleep again? What's Alice doing in my home?

I found my way downstairs, one step at a time. The coffee pot was off, the beans crushed and still inside the filter. I reached inside the coffee pot to toss the coffee grains into the trash and smelled cigarettes instead. Someone had been in the house. David doesn't smoke. Neither do I.
I admire the blue-gray granite countertops in our kitchen. Why didn't I notice that before?

The cat balls. The cat balls lay in their usual spot under the chair on the floor. Kelly. Where's Kelly the cat? Perhaps if I turn them on, I can get a reply from Alice. Perhaps Kelly will come dashing in to say good evening. Whatever would make it less silent, I would welcome. If only I can lean down to grab them, that would make my day. Go on, make my day, said Arnold. Or was it Clint Eastwood who said that line? Grab those cat balls. You can do it.

I spot a cane leaning against the wall, then the walker they gave me. Steel, not too chic, just plain old steel like those you see in older folk's homes. You need them, Michelle. Your mom uses one. Don't be like that.

I grab the cane and try to move one cat ball to the stair step. Up one. Up two. Up three and maybe I can lean down enough just to grab one and turn it on. Alice, I hope it's you. Did you smoke?

259

I nudge the cat ball with the cane and of course it slides off. It falls and rolls across the floor towards the kitchen. It stops by a stool leg. I nudge the other cat ball, just against the wall and push it towards the stairs. One more time. I concentrate, sweat with the effort, steeling myself to be patient. Let's do this. I just have to turn on that switch if I can just reach it.

The ball slides, but not in the direction I wanted it to. I nudge it with my feet, sort of between my toes to coax it up towards the steps, using the cane for support. There. I kick it and it bounces up one step. Thank goodness for carpeting. The carpet's so clean like it was new.

I now have the ball on one step, but still can't lean far enough forward with the brace on. The cell dings upstairs. Dang it. I forgot to bring it down with me. I wonder who's texting. Must be David as he's due home any minute. Oh my gosh. I missed my PT appointment.

So strange. He gets up, goes down to make coffee and next thing you know it's twilight outside. I really did miss out on a lot of sleep. I meant, the entire time my back was hurting I really couldn't get a straight good night's rest. After the prison visit, it was worse. I now recall something causing me to stir in the middle of the night.

Back to the ball. One more step, then another until it's level with me. I raise my foot, leaning on the cane. I nudge it. Oops. It's down on the floor again, darn it. I breath and exhale, hoping I don't lose my patience. I look outside and it's now completely dark. Where's David? I turn back to the ball.

Wait. The ball was up on the lowest step. Or was it? No, it had come down again. No, wait. This is another ball, now resting next to my foot. How'd it get there? I see the ball I'd been trying to move up the step. Maybe Alice is trying to help me. I just need verification that she's present. I have to call Jane, plan to see her as part of my healing. She really helps.

260

Wait. The third ball is here too. Didn't realize it was by my other foot. I nudge the first ball with my foot and it rolls away. I follow it.

A click. Something shifts. I am dizzy.

The ball pauses and stops next to a foot with boots on. I feel my skin prickle. It's not David.
Slowly, I raise my head, the pain in my neck subsiding with the effort. It's the stitches now, not the neck that's hurting. I think I overexerted. I look up and I am backing away, backing away, backing away.

A man. A faceless man with a hat like a fedora is in my kitchen. I smell the sulfur. His eyes are red pinpricks. The silence in the room is complete.

"Get out! Get out in the name of God." I heard myself screaming, yelling and slamming my hand on the granite kitchen counter by the window. The man laughs a horrific laugh as if he's gone mad. It's a maniacal laugh I will never forget.

I hear myself scream and the cat balls all go off in unison. I turn to the back door to dash out and run into Kelly, screeching as she madly dashed out into the lawn ahead of me.
"Kelly! Kelly! Come!"
I dart after her before she got to the street and into traffic. I slam head on onto someone's chest.
I look up and it's none other than David.
"What the heck is going on? Michelle? You shouldn't be running like this."

David grabs Kelly, placing her under one arm with practiced effort. He takes me by one arm and escorts me back towards the house. It is daytime. I look down at my watch which was on my wrist the entire time.

It was seven thirty in the morning. What's happening here?

## **Chapter Forty Seven**

You think you can stop me? I am in the house and Alice can't do a thing about it. Paul and Clementine can't do anything about it. You can't stop me. There's many out there that think they can. I am better than them. I am wise and powerful and I can outwit you all. Ha ha ha. Time as your closet phantom Paul said before, doesn't matter. Here where I am, where that fool Paul is, where his victim is… or was, I should say since you crossed her over, has no time to be concerned about either. That's a human thing. Like death. We are timeless.

To you I bestow the angel of fear. Ha ha ha. You just have no idea how things can seem so unreal. You think your clairvoyance can help much? Want more pain in your behind? I could be a pain, I know. I could be your forever pain if you don't stop being so damn kind. We don't like that.

Try it again. Try and reach Alice. She's scared of me. She was in life and now in death, she still is. That bitch. I truly am getting tired of her. I thought I got rid of her once and for all and guess I didn't. Now she's trying to warn you about me and what I am about to do to Julia.
Henry's outside Julia's house. Ha. Ha. Julia who thought she could escape Henry the hubby. No, Julia. Your sister can't protect you from Henry. I got Henry's back and we're going to do you good like I did with Alice. Guess what? After that, I have no further use for Henry. Sitting out there in the woods, watching and getting weathered, no food, no water. Bad for Henry, but not for me. I'm an eternal pain in the ass and Henry will be too - soon. He will join our ranks in the eternal.

Baby? Who cares. It's Henry's bastard. You think he loves it? Nah ah. No, I don't think so and I am about to prove it. I sent Henry to the address. You see, I can see what you can't. I know where her sister lives. Now where do you think you're going? I fixed your back. The good ol' doc can't figure out what happened there. That rod failed cause of me. Pushed you psychically like it was literally a train running alongside you, derailing you, so to speak.

Well, well, well. What will you do next? I know what I'm doing. I am going to set about moving Henry around like a manikin that he is. Poor thing. So corruptible, so stupid and so angry and miserable. It serves him right.

Yeah, I use people. So what. I did before, why change now? There's nothing to it. You like my hat? You didn't see my cape? Yeah, it's designed to scare the shit tit out of you stupid women. Shit tit. Shit tit. Shit tit. Ha ha ha.

I am going to make some interesting things happen. Going in the house now.

264

265

## **Chapter Forty Eight**

In a daze, Michelle prepares for her physical therapist. She detects from the voice on the phone that it's a young woman. Solicitous, wishing to please and friendly. Despite that, she seems very businesslike, Michelle thought, on the phone. She detected a faint New England accent. Clipped, fast and efficient. She was her first appointment at ten, the first of ten visits to the house, then she would be driving to the outpatient office. Where is she from? Why did she move here?

Despite the highly strange event of the morning, Michelle tries to relax, take her time as she warms up for her exercise routine she learned while at the rehab wing of the hospital. She was glad in a way the physical therapist was coming, though the vibe of the house appeared different today. She hopes nothing else would happen to unsettle her, and the young woman who sounded so young and naive. Not a midwesterner, Michelle gleans from her clipped accent.

Michelle surveys the room for the cat balls and spots them, all three, in a corner of the formal dining table. The house was quiet in a surreal way that she could not wrap her head around. Michelle prayed quietly, asking for assistance on the outcome of the visit and for a peace to resume in her abode. Then, as if to answer, Kelly the cat darted in and rubbed herself against Michelle's legs, purring. The cat was a signal that everything was okay as cats were traditionally protectors of homes and their owners. Michelle exhales and sighs with relief. She recalls Kelly dashing out in terror with Michelle right behind.

Not willing to give up on Alice, she decides she would ask the young woman when she arrived to pick up the cat balls for her. She could check their batteries and turn them on after the appointment was over. Now knowing Alice, she would reply immediately and make herself known with her perfume. She thought she had smelled verbena, Alice's trademark perfume, but it was cigarette smoke this morning that came with the phantom who confronted her at arms' length. She could only hope nothing malevolent had followed her home, but the worry lingered in the calm of daylight. Then, she recalls the prison.

Michelle continues to pray as she sat and waited at the dining table. Earlier, her mind was in a flux as she grappled with how to tell her husband that she was caught in a time warp of sorts, perhaps even a portal where the house was transported to a later time at night. On the spur of the moment, she decided not to tell David about the presence in the house which appeared to be able to manipulate time as she knew it.

David was a believer, but the paranormal to him was an abstraction. Her story would only worry him when his work was enough to occupy his mind. David and Jake: The two men in her life who kept her in check in three dimensional reality with its density, pragmatism and the Occam's Razor principle - search for explanations constructed with the most possible set of elements. Down to earth men like her father, whose principled ways and sense of integrity marshaled them into a trustworthy and successful family.

She stares at the vials of medicine she was taking and wondered if there was anything hallucinogenic as a side effect in one of the pain killers. However, she had passed that point of needing to take any pain killers. She spots her kitchen crucifix staring back at her from the kitchen wall opposite. Michelle turns in her chair and prays for help in alleviating the confusion that lingered. As she went deeper into a prayer state, the flux that came to unsettle her nerves were finally dissipating. She felt her back ease despite the staples and brace that held her with determination.

Michelle finally opens her eyes, drawn to the wall of framed family photos by the credenza. One, a young man in his twenties; Ron at a graduation ceremony, then a group photo of her with her brothers as children. Rob, the oldest at forty, on a

267

separate frame with a wide smile. His eyes focused on Michelle, her grief flooding suddenly at his unexpected loss to cancer.

Rob, the clairvoyant.

Suddenly, her mind cleared like a pond to the bottom where the Koi created a chiaroscuro of orange and beige. A light came on in her mind: Something akin to a eureka experience. No, that was not a time warp. She heard water. The cleansing flow of clear water.

It was precognition. Something was coming to the house later.
Something unclean, unholy and full of hate.
A lesser entity. She sees and recalls the fedora hat.
She looks up to the sound of an engine.

Michelle stood as a blue late model Chevy SUV pulls up and parks on the driveway. A young woman in her twenties exits the car. Michelle looks down at her watch: 11:11.
Her mind floods with the encounter of the morning:

She was definitely not home.
Kelly the cat wasn't there because Michelle was at someone else's house.
The cat would be home in her own kitchen. Michelle wasn't in her own kitchen.
The kitchen had no island and the countertops were a grey/blue marbled granite, whereas hers was tile. White tile. She was in someone else's house. She had just seen what was happening to someone else. Who?

The young woman approaches the front door, pushing her hair back from her face like Julia did despite the pony tail. Stray hairs on her forehead bothered Julia like this woman in an athletic outfit was doing. She was pushing tendrils of hair off her face. A habit Julia had.

268

Michelle scanned in her memory the color of the house when she exited to get away from the phantom with the scowl and laugh, leering at her, wearing boots. Michelle's house had yellow trim with white siding. The house she exited earlier was a light blue with white trim.

The doorbell rang and Michelle stood, now in alarm.
Something malevolent was approaching a house. Not Michelle's, but someone else's house.
This young woman had Julia's face.

Michelle tries to recall the color of Julia's house, just yards from the penitentiary's walls. Red. The house's siding was barn red which matched the garage. Not Julia's house.

Michelle dashes out the front door, out the front walk and almost runs into the young woman. Now Michelle realizes why she had the physical therapy today. Why did the physical therapist look so familiar? She was a doppelgänger for Julia. Julia's eyes, face, even her hair, despite that fact that was a younger version.

"Are you Julia's sister?"
The young woman stepped back, pushing her hair off her face.
"Julia Sargent? Yes." The New England accent. Julia came from Massachusetts.
"Glad to meet you."
"Oh, you're the same Michelle that she talks about. Small world."
"Is she still staying with you?"
"Yes, she is."
"What color is your house?"
"Beg your pardon?"
"What color is your house?"
"Blue. Blue siding with white trim. Why?"
Silence. How do you tell a stranger you just met?
"She may be in danger. Something may happen this afternoon or evening."

269

"You mean the husband? Henry has a restraining order."

"I know but that won't help." Michelle hurriedly rushes back into the house, the therapist in tow.

"I'm Pam, by the way." The young woman yells as she follows Michelle into the house.

Michelle nods, acknowledging Pam. Pam sits on the sofa, discomfited. She has a gym bag with her as if she had just returned from Planet Fitness. Pam surveys her surroundings as Michelle dials her cell phone.

The cell rings.

"Tell me again what your house looks like. Please."

Pam pauses. She gives Michelle a puzzled look. Silence.

"Tell me so I know I'm not dreaming."

"It's blue siding with white trim. Sits on a half-acre of land by the…"

"Your kitchen?"

"Uh, granite counters in, uh, a blue-gray, white cabinets… is that what you mean?"

"Yes."

The cell continues to ring.

"She's not answering. Your sister - did she go somewhere this morning?"

"Yes. As a matter of fact, she went back to her house to get some of her boxes. She still has…"

"Right now?"

"Well, this morning, before I could get ready… she should be back by now."

Pam digs into her bag, reveals her cell phone and dials. She places it on her ear. Ringing.

"I'll try again in the few minutes." Pam disconnects her phone. "She's not answering."

Michelle ushers Pam into the dining room where she left a sheaf of papers - her exercise directions. She pulls a dining chair and sits as Pam positions her gym bag on the floor, unzipping it.

"I think it followed her."

"Who?"

"Whatever was in her house followed her to yours."

Pam's eyes turn wide.

"What are you talking about?"

"Whatever is happening to Henry…"

"Henry's at my house?  How do you know?"

271

272

## **<u>Chapter Forty Nine</u>**

"You have to believe me. Your sister shouldn't have gone back to the house. I really think it's followed her."
"You're not serious. This can't be."
"Please call someone. I don't know what's happening there."
"She's probably fine. She locks all the doors. It's late and I have another patient after you."
"I just think I need to go to your house and get her out of there for now."
"How would you know? Henry doesn't know where I live."
"She went back without anyone with her?"
"No. She alerted the police. They're not going to go with her every time she gets her stuff."
"It's not Henry. Please. Call her again."

Pam takes out several plastic straps, extending them.
"I need this green one around your foot. We'll do sitting exercises first."
"Pam… I know you're on the clock… but this is your sister."
"She's fine. Please."
"I need to warn you."
"She's fine. I'll call again as soon as you're set up here."

Michelle places the green elastic around her sneaker and moves as instructed as Pam busies herself setting about the equipment around the large dining room. The large bay window lighted the entire room, suffusing the area with natural light. Michelle glances at her family photos on the wall as she counts off her reps.
"The sooner you get well, the better you'll feel. Then you can do anything you like."
"I meant, I just am really concerned about what might be happening to your sister."
The girl pauses.

273

"I know you mean well, but I think Julia sometimes just believes in this stuff too much."

Michelle sighs, standing to do the next exercise. Behind Pam, she spots her three cat balls by the dining table. Alice. She needs Alice.

"Do you mind picking those balls up behind you, please?"

Pam straightens from scribbling on her chart and eyes the balls behind her. She hurriedly retrieves them and places them on the dining table. She returns to the exercise routine.

"For this one, Michelle. I need you to stand by the table and raise one leg at a time." Pam retrieves the straps and places them back into her duffel bag. She searches, rummaging inside the bag.

Michelle stands and grabs each cat ball and turns them on. She places them in a fruit bowl in the center of the dining table. The batteries were on full power. She sighs.

"Try not to lean forward. Your braces are still on. Put your hand on the chair back and raise your foot like these. Do twenty reps for each one, please."


Michelle begins, looking out the dining room window. It was noon and the school bus drove by. An early dismissal day.

"Ten. Do another ten."

The room dims. A cloud passes, a sign of a storm to come.

Pam glances out the window as she prompts Michelle to start the other foot.

"One, two. One, two."

The cat passes, pauses and hisses.

Pam looks down as Kelly darts out of the room.

"One, two. One, two." Michelle continues, mentally trying to communicate with Alice.

One cat ball lights up. It moves and rolls off the bowl and onto the the dining table.

Pam looks down, staring at the lighted ball as it flickers.

"Neat."

274

Another cat ball lights up and flickers. It rolls off the table, joining the other on the carpeted floor.

Pam looks down again, puzzled.

"Interesting."

"One, two. One, two." Michelle says, her eyes far away. Alice.

The last cat ball lights green. It rolls towards the edge of the table and falls to the carpeted floor, joining the other two. Three independent verifications.

"Alice!" Michelle whispers in triumph. "One, two, one two. Done."

Pam stands and stares at the cat balls, all lighting green and flashing in unison.

"What's making those…" Suddenly, she looks out the window, confused and stunned. "What is that?"

Michelle follows Pam's line of sight. "Am I doing the other foot?" Michelle asks.

One, two. One, two. Michelle pauses.

Pam appears mesmerized, her eyes focusing on something across the street. A large black blob.

The area perceptibly darkens as if a shower was about to pour down. A rumble. Thunder.

Lightning lights up the sky.

"Another of those sudden storms we tend to have here."

"We have them in New England too."

A silhouette takes shape. Rain obliterates the view as the water comes down in sheets. Thrumming rain. Beyond the rain, the shape of a man with a hat. It skims towards the grass and onto the yard. Towards the dining room window. He seemed faceless, skimming the surface of grass as rain began to hail down in sheets.

Michelle touches Pam's shoulder. "Don't go anywhere. He's back."

"Who? Who's back?"

"Him."

275

Pam breaks her reverie and bolts for the front door. Locked. She looks up as Michelle continues to watch the man approaching the dining room window. It was as if he was oblivious to the pouring rain. The same man who confronted her this morning.

Michelle darts for her cell on the bed upstairs. "I'll be back."

"You're back! Don't bend. You can't bend!" Pam follows up the stairs in pursuit.

Michelle was already on her cell phone.

"Julia, please call me. Please."

"What's this got to do with my sister?"

"What did you see?"

"Outside?"

"Yes. Just now."

"A mini tornado? Is that what it is?"

"That's not what I saw."

The cell clicks.

Someone hung up.


Michelle dashes down and heads for the front door.

"What are you doing? Don't you think we should stay inside? Your basement?" Pam yells.

"Don't believe what you see. Please!"

Despite her back brace and the stitches still in repair, Michelle darts for the front door, twisting the handle open.


The door opens in a whoosh. Light. Sunlight. Michelle steps out.

He's playing with both of them to keep them away. Away from Julia, Michelle gathers.

"Let's go. Put your stuff away. I need you to drive me to a friend's house. My sound healer."

"Sound what?"

Michelle rushes past an awestruck Pam and runs up the stairs again.

"Your brace! You can't bend!"

276

"I have to get my medals and the holy water.  Help me!"
Pam dashes up the steps.

Michelle runs into the bedroom.  In a corner, she spots her duffel bag just where David had left it. Pam enters as Michelle points.  "Please check what's inside.  I meant, I need some things to be in there."

277

278

## **<u>Chapter Fifty</u>**

Where are you now, Michelle? Still playing with fire? I am right outside the house. You gave me a reason to disturb the seamless fabric of their lives, sending spirits to the brightness of your God. Now, you're going to suffer the consequences for letting souls cross over. I am the disruptor, the despair in the back of people's minds, including yours. I am the one who steals into your sleep thus while you dream, I turn it into a nightmare. If you're ill, I lead you to the tower of despair as you claw your way inch by inch to what you hope is wellness.

I dissuade people from truth and promote what you call ignorance. I keep them wrapped in their lack of knowledge, insight and of course, foresight. I discourage those who have intuition. I am a lot like you with your prowess for knowing who is in the room who is not in this dimension of yours. However, I know you and others better than themselves.

Now we must address your goal. Those who help you must be stopped, discouraged, led to helplessness. Ready? Where do you think you're going, you bitch. Why is Alice with you? It's too late. I'm in the house.

I see you've successfully recruited Paul and even that young girl whose life he destroyed. I see they're in the light. I'm not going there. I am afraid of the light. No, sister. No lights for me. What is Paul and Clementine suppose to do? Who are they? I don't know either one and I knew Alice in life. But who is she that I should be afraid of her too? You're silly. This is a mere playground you're creating.

That sound woman? Who is she? I don't know here either. No idea who you're bringing around to defeat me. Us. I am sorry for you. So powerless like Henry. So pathetic. All I have to do is muddle your mind. You don't even know where you are and what I can do to confuse the jeebies out of you. You and that lot of women.

Foolish. You're still healing you know.

280

## **Chapter Fifty One**

Julia turns the car into the second garage, hitting the remote her sister had just given to her. The garage door with a pretty design for windows smoothly moves upward, the stark white a contrast to the robin's egg blue siding. Julia makes a mental note to buy some flowers and maybe plant a pot of yellow and blue flowers by the garage to complement it while she was there.

Pam had invited her to stay for as long as she needed, while she attempts to complete her divorce and locate another home. Julia decided with all the terrifying things going on in the house that she couldn't imagine staying another night even with Henry gone, if he agrees to move. She had no idea where he was or if he was still living on the property, sleeping in the garage where the hauntings began.

Julia decided she had to muster up the courage to go to her house and collect what was left of her clothes. She had to pack some items which were dear to her: Her mother's collection of jewelry which was willed to her, her antique vases from the house in Massachusetts and other heirlooms. Pam would never forgive her if she had left them. She finally had them all now, despite her fear of encountering Henry, who fortunately wasn't anywhere in the house. If he had been, she wouldn't enter after filing a restraining order. She wouldn't have dared without a police escort, but no one was available that morning and she didn't want to wait on getting the precious items.

Taking much longer to pack than she expected, Julia had lovingly wrapped each vase for the transport into Pam's house. She didn't dare break these treasures nor forget the jewelry from their mother. While she packed, she surveyed and listened for footsteps, a car door, or any evidence of Henry. After the terrifying incident involving Michelle, she was afraid of what may come out of the woods. Filled with trepidation, Julia had pushed a chair against both the front and back doors,

282

also squeamish of any rats hiding in the corners after the incident with the grille. She noted the garage doors were left open, but slightly, the heavy doors ajar as if in wait. She sighed knowing there was nothing in the garage she needed, having brought all the boxes with her from the local wine store.

Finally back in Pam's house, Julia exits the car, spots the side door leading into the kitchen and finds herself in the coolness of the spotless kitchen with a granite island. The soft hues of gray/blue countertops gleam in the soft light of late afternoon. A contrast to the white glass-front cabinets, Pam made a point to exude her personal style of calm and orderliness in her new home. Despite having to move to the midwest to accept a job offer, she was glad when Julia's husband also moved them to the same area, if not the same state the next town over. It was luck in Julia's mind. They only had each other.

The stillness wraps Julia in a cocoon of comfort. She picks up a Le Creuset teapot in French blue and fills it with water for tea on the tap. The water gushes through a soft-water filter, as she marveled at the contraptions her sister could afford. Her home was shabby and outdated compared to hers. A pang of envy hits her and a sense of resentment builds of the past she shared with Henry whose spotty employ landed them the old and haunted house they live in.

As the kettle fills, Julia absently gazes at the tile backsplash in a mosaic pattern. A pattern reminiscent of Moorish Spain. She shuts off the water in time to hear footsteps above her.
She listens, wondering who was upstairs. She sets the kettle on the stove, also in a blue tone that matched the mosaic blue tiles. She turns on the gas flame.
Footsteps. The floorboards creak above her head.
Julia recalls her sister's floors were all handsomely made with hardwood. The house was too new to creak like an old one, but she wonders if Pam had come home early from her patient appointments.

She walks slowly as she waits for the kettle to boil towards the door leading back to the garage. She opens it and notes only her car is in the garage.

Footsteps. Whoever it is, is headed towards the stairs.

284

## **Chapter Fifty Two**

Jane places her drum and sticks onto the back of the Chevy SUV. Beside it was Michelle's duffel bag. She turns and surveys the neighborhood, sensing the calmness before the storm. They were expecting a storm to head their way, possibly even a tornado in its wake. She approaches her house, checking the windows, closing the shutters one by one. Finally satisfied, she enters the back door and makes her way to the front of the house where Michelle sits with a young woman in her small sitting room. The young woman appears distraught, as if the carpet had been pulled from under her.

"Let's assume the worse and plan for the worse, but hope for the best as they say." Michelle nods as she hands Jane a rosary. They sit in a circle with the coffee table littered with saint's medals. A vial of holy water with a label sits nearby.
"I am not a practicing Roman Catholic, I have to admit. I may not remember…" Pam followed.
"We'll lead you and you can just follow. No worries on that." Michelle offered. Michelle and Jane bowed and they began in earnest with the Saint Micheal prayer and then one with Padre Pio.
"So you and Jane are doing a combo ritual of sorts … using drums too?" Pam interrupts.
"Yes. It addresses the Masters and the Indian guides at the same time."
"How does this kind of town react to that?" Pam mused out loud. "I'm just saying. To combine Christianity with American Indian…"
"It's whatever works. How everyone reacts is different." Jane responded.
 "How God reacts is what matters." Michelle adds.
Michelle looks up and sees a visage, an apparition in translucence. Alice. Alice smiles from the corner of the room. The cat balls seem to be accurate.
She bows her head and continues praying out loud, the chanting from the three women enveloping the room with calm.

286

The scent of lily of the valley and verbena permeate the room.

"Harry has placed a curse on the land." Michelle mumbles, voicing an intuition, an unseen communication:

Michelle, it's Mary Michelle. The Indian guides are there now trying to help you by cleansing the ground. He still has a hold on Henry. He is upstairs with Henry. In Pam's house.

Yes. He's in Pam's house. The curse is on Pam's house. Harry is trying to drive Julia back to her home. Alice agrees, a voice in Michelle's mind.

It's Paul. Harry is going to drive Julia away from her sister's, so she can be imprisoned in her own home, her site of misery. Do you hear me, Michelle?

Michelle opens her eyes. Both Jane and Pam were studying her. "I'm hearing a lot."
"Huh?" Pam's eyes lock on Michelle's.
"Oh, gosh. We're glad you're back. You were in a trance." Jane announces, her hands in the air.
"Let's go. They're in your house, Pam."
"What?"
"Go. I have to take all the Saint Micheal medals." Michelle sits up as Pam reaches for her arm to support her, watching the brace on the woman's back.

287

288

## <u>Chapter Fifty Three</u>

Julia dashes to the living room, her eyes trained on the stairs. She turns and looks up the stairs. Where the top of the stairs is usually lighted by a window above, there was darkness. Someone was moving up there, getting closer to the stairs.
"Pam? Is that you?"
Silence.
A chuckle.
"Who's there?"
The tea kettle whistles. A shrill noise, breaking the silence.
Julia dashes back to the kitchen, taking the kettle off the stove. She shuts off the pilot in time to hear
A creak.
Someone was at the head of the stairs. She hears a creak, then a breath.
A shadow, rising from the floor. Julia's eyes widen. She gasps.
A nebulous dark cloud takes shape in the dim light of the upstairs landing.
"Oh, God."
Julia's arms prickle, the room suddenly plummeting down to frost. She sees her own breathe.
Rooted to the ground, unable to move, Julia fights to run.
The shadow forms into a man in silhouette. A silhouette with a fedora hat. Eyes. Red. Aflame.
A snicker issues from the silhouette.
One foot in boots steps down one step.
Towards Julia.

Julia bolts.

289

Julia dashes for the front door, moves the chair away and trips on the chair's leg. She struggles to get up and pulls. The door is locked. She unlocks it, but it keeps locking. Click. Click. Click. Click.
Julia pulls in vain as she watches the black silhouette descend in booted steps down the stairs. One, two. One, two. One foot. Then the other.
It was halfway down.

Julia dashes for the dining room, sees the skylight darken above her like a tornado in its wake.
The room darkens as she struggles to go around the table and into the kitchen.
In the kitchen she sees the knives lined magnetically on a strip on the wall.
She grabs one and turns, spotting the booted shadow walk on the floor.
Creak.
Creak.
Back into the dining room. The shifting form in boots is coming.

Julia bolts for the kitchen door. The back door. She pulls the chair away.
Outside, through the kitchen door's pane, she spots the darkened area around the house - wind swirling leaves into a funnel.
"Oh, no."
She pulls the door open with a whoosh.
She runs against the wind to the front of the house.
Julia pauses, taking in the garage door.
She squats, grabs the garage door latch and pulls it up.
Again.
Again.
She strains as the wind blows her hair, disengaging her pony tail.
The door won't budge.
"No. Please."

Julia dashes back to the kitchen door - wide open. As she enters she brandishes the knife as if fighting off an invisible assailant. The house is completely dark.

"I've got a knife!"

A chuckle.

"What do you want from me?"

A breathe. Something is breathing near her ear.
Julia quickly turns, the knife now in both hands.

Julia feels her stomach. A mild pain within. The baby.
Realization dawns on Julia's face.
"No, you're not going to get her!"

Another breath. "Go away."

Julia dashes for the kitchen door and it opens with a whoosh before she could reach
for the knob.
She exits and bolts to the front of the house. Wind pummels her hair, her face, her
arms wildly moving with a knife clutched in one hand. She turns and finds the
garage door is open by some miracle.

"Fine. I'll get out of here if you don't follow me." Julia whispers to the phantom
she can't see.
She leaps into her car, tossing the knife in the seat. The engine revs as she pulls
the car in reverse, burning rubber as she goes down the street. Rain descends.

Within the car, Julia glances at the rearview mirror. On the pavement stands the
silhouette, hatted, grinning with glee.

291

292

## **<u>Chapter Fifty Four</u>**

"Stand in a circle. Ignore the wind." Michelle yells, her hair plastered on her face. They link hands, creating a triangle. Wind steadily blows as leaves form a circle around them and trees sway.
"You're crazy!" Pam yells. "No, she's not." Jane retorts.
Michelle shuts her eyes and chants a prayer. Jane joins in.

The wind blows steadily, knocking down trash bins nearby. They roll towards the group. Tree limbs creak. Some crack and fall around them. They continue to chant in prayer, ignoring the outer weather as their inner weather takes hold.

"Calm. Take the curse away, Lord God." Jane chants.
"In you, we trust and place our faith in." Michelle chants.
Pam repeats the chant and Michelle adds the Saint Micheal prayer.
"Let's say the rosary. Again." Michelle shuts her eyes against the wind, the rain now driving in sheets.
"Oh, it's getting worse." Pam adds. She attempts to break away and the wind howls.
"Come back. Faith. Have faith." Michelle prods Pam.
They chant.

Minutes pass.

The wind passes.

Tree limbs bend, leaves scintillate: the breeze coming in gentle waves. The chill remains in the air as the storm abates to a gentle rain.

Jane opens her eyes and points to the back yard. "Your yard?"

293

Without a word, Pam leads them to the back yard and the women set up their drums.

With a trowel, Michelle walks to the edge of the property and points to the ground, her movements restricted by her back. Jane grabs the trowel and digs. She makes a hole about a half foot deep and Michelle tosses a saint's medal into the hole, as Jane buries it. Michelle chants a prayer to Saint Micheal, the Archangel. She rushes to the opposite side where there's a home past a fence. By the fence, Jane digs and repeats the process. Michelle chants a second prayer to another saint, Saint Pio. She does the same to the front two sides.

Done with the medals, soaked to the bone, Michelle joins Jane on the wet grass, sitting cross legged across from each other. Muddied and wet, they drum an ancient American Indian drum roll to fend off the entities that may inhabit the area. They had sealed the property on four sides with the energy of the saints' medals and are now drumming out whatever remained.

The sound of drumming permeates the area, taking hold, changing the mood. Another hour passes.

Suddenly, the chill and breeze cease and the shower abates. They look up at the sky as Pam gasps, shivering as she stands observing the process. The clouds dissipate.

Inside, the kitchen lights wink on. Then the living room and the upper floors.

"Go inside." Michelle whispers to Pam. "It came from the roof and was at the top of the stairs." Pam leaves Michelle's side who continues to play the drums in harmony with Jane. "Am I okay to go in alone?" Michelle nods as she plays. "Grab the vial of holy water. Sprinkle it on all sides of each room."

294

Inside the house, Pam opens a vial of holy water, reading a blessing from Saint Pio. She waves the vial towards the four sides of each room and finally goes up the stairs where unbeknownst to her, Julia had seen the formless void take form. The house regained its warmth. The thermostat on the wall indicated a comfortable seventy degrees .

The house had changed its mood. Pam could feel it a difference she'd never felt before.

Outside, Michelle and Jane wipe their faces and their drums. Above them, a rainbow stretches as the trees glimmer with wet leaves. Jane helps Michelle up and studies Pam as she approaches with the vial of holy water, still in her hand. She appeared bewildered, in disbelief.
"Your faith has saved your house. Don't undo it with doubt." Michelle comments as she watches the young woman's reaction.

"Let's go. We must get to Julia now." Jane dashes for the car as the two women follow.

295

296

## **<u>Chapter Fifty Five</u>**

The walls of the house appears red to Julia as she approaches the front door. One porch light was still on from when she had left it in haste that morning, but the other appears to be out. It made the house even more off-kilter, the one lamp remaining flickers as if ready to give up. As she inserts her key, the lamp's bulb finally winks out, plummeting her in darkness. The storm had abated, but with it was a hollowness, a sense of emptiness, like the litter of old newspapers left by a neighbor to flutter and spread on the street and onto the grass.

The grass had been left to neglect, wild and overgrown. It was obvious Henry had not been home to mow his precious lawn which had been his pride earlier in the marriage when they moved. Despite the several months of marital strife, a part of Julia still cared and she wondered where he was.

Julia peers in an adjacent window as the door gives way to a steady hum of something indeterminate. The walls, painted a butternut yellow and gaily wallpapered in the hall with small poppies in a sea of light green appears faded and gaudy. The butternut yellow appears to be mustard now and where the living room yields to the deeper recesses of the dining area and kitchen, it looked crimson. Like blood.

As she listens, Julia determines the low hum evinces from deeper, somewhere within the house. That sound wasn't there earlier while she packed. She wondered if Henry had been or is still inside the house now. Where was the sound coming from?
Mentally, Julia scrolls through what she may have left on, but knew she had touched nothing else but the jewelry and antiques. She wouldn't have dared to do anything else in her haste to be done and out. Now she was back, compelled to return by the presence in Pam's house.

297

Perhaps the kitchen. Julia shoulders her bag more tightly as if someone would pick it off her shoulder. Keys in hand, she reaches to the back pocket of her jeans for the knife she had found in her sister's kitchen. The solid blade of stainless steel gleamed despite the fading light of day as if attempting to give off light in the despondent gloom.

The kitchen light is on. Past the stove, she notes the basement door is ajar. The hum was stronger here, issuing from the basement. Julia gropes for the light switch on the wall on the right side, her right hand clutching the knife. She pockets it into the back of her jeans and flicks the switch up.

Someone had left the dryer on. Henry had probably returned to grab whatever he could while she busied herself gathering boxes at the liquor store. She realizes he still had his keys to the back door. Julia ponders when he could have returned, feeling stalked more than ever as she had arrived earlier that day to get her treasures. She surmised he had ventured in after watching her leave. She resolved to check his side of the closet and then pack them herself. Perhaps she'd meet him or drop off whatever belongings remained in a public area.

Julia steps down the stairs, in pregnant wait for something to spring at her. She felt taut as a drawstring, afraid the stress would make her lose the child growing inside her. She exhales with effort, noting that the dryer was banging against something on the wall as it rotated. The scent of something putrid assailed her nostrils, making her gag. Something raw, rancid, spoiled. It was akin to rotten meat, she decided. She braces for whatever was in the dryer, stealing glances around the walls of the unfinished basement, ready for something or someone to dart out at her. It was the last place she wanted to be.

The dryer had clothing. Towels, shorts, shirts, it appeared. A pair of sneakers. That explained the hum and the banging. Henry had been in that basement as recent as forty minutes ago when the cycle had begun, according to the dryer's

298

dial. She was at Pam's by then, she concluded. She wonders what could have been so important for him to do his wash and dry. That would also mean he would be returning for his clean laundry, perhaps in a few minutes.

Panic seized Julia at the thought of Henry's imminent return as she realized she was in the basement that had no exit that she knew of. Then, further down the cement floor, she spots another knife, similar to Pam's. Like the one in her back pocket.

A click. Something shifts in Julia's consciousness.

Julia approaches the knife and leans down to pick it up. The knife was slick with blood. She gasps, dropping it. She stares at her hand, now wet. Fresh blood. She wipes it on her jeans, now with growing unease.

She opens the dryer, which is now a wooden barrel of sorts, like one would find in a flea market or antique shop.

Clothes fall on the floor. Mostly Henry's as she surmised, but not those she'd seen him wear.

A heavy cotton towel, stained with blood, a shirt with strange buttons, almost vintage, also stained. Blood doesn't come off easily even when placed quickly in the wash. She wonders as she stares at the articles of clothing what Henry had been doing. The stains were huge, as if someone had been stabbed or worse. The shoes - boots she'd never seen before, except at the antiques store in town: stained with red. Blood stains.

Julia leaves the clothes on the cement floor, backing away, alarm and confusion on her face. Then, she darts back, placing them back in the - barrel. She didn't want Henry to notice she had been touching his clothes or that she had made some discovery that he would not want revealed. The clothes appear outdated, worn but made by hand.

She straightens and her eyes catch a door she had not noticed before. It was sat recessed beyond the stall where they kept the old furniture from the previous owner stashed, forgotten and never picked up. She approaches as she grabs the knife from her back pocket, slowly inching her way towards the wooden door.

She reaches for the brass knob, noting a keyhole beneath. The keyhole and the knob appeared antique. She peers in.

300

## Chapter Fifty Six

"Help me with the door." Michelle pushes with one shoulder. It wouldn't budge. Jane pushes. Pam approaches from the front path. "Let me try."
Pam kicks the front door open, the knob giving way. A chair had been anchored under the knob from inside. "Julia?"

The three women enter, noting the house seemed eerily silent. "Where did she go?" Pam darted from room to room, now in alarm. Then, she heard a humming sound below the house. "The basement."

Michelle scans the house, taking in the mood. Something bad had happened while they were at Pam's. It may be too late. She reaches for her cell phone in her handbag. She dials. "Let's go out to the car together and protect ourselves before we do anything."
"What if she's hurt?" Pam retorts with anxiety.
"We can't do anything for her unless we're protected."

The three rush out as Michelle talks on the phone. "Hey, how many can you gather to come right now to Julia's house?" She listens. "I think something just happened. Let's pray first when you all arrive."
Jane brings out a Saint Micheal medal and a prayer card. "Anyone else available?"
"Yes. Some are just home from work now."
Several minutes later, Michelle's cell rings. "Okay. We're going to start praying."
Michelle enters Pam's car and they pray while they wait. It was close to six pm.

Three vehicles arrive. Michelle's grown children, Jessica and Jake emerge from one vehicle. Then the others emerge, including Nancy. Curbside, the group assembles, joining hands in a circle.

302

"Let's do it, team. Julia and Henry are not here that I can feel. Something just happened here and it could get dangerous. Before I survey what's going on, let's do a circle of protection. I have to decide whether it's safe for everyone to enter."

"Saint Micheal, defend us in battle..."
The team followed, reciting the prayer out loud with linked hands as they stand in a circle.

"We believe in you Lord God... Almighty and powerful..."

"Look!" Nancy yells, as she faces the house in the circle. "There's something in there."
Michelle turns in time to see a shadow standing at the window.
"Let's go in." Pam yells.
"No, not yet. Wait until I tell you it's safe."

This time, Michelle places the blessed rosary beads around her neck and opens the vial of holy water. The curtain closes where Nancy had seen the shadow.
Car doors open. Behind Michelle the team disperses with efficiency, bringing out the paranormal equipment, ready for a possible investigation with evidence. They await Michelle's instructions.

Trees bend to a stiff wind. Michelle stands in the center of the lawn, this time looking at the tree line where she had been confronted before. This time, the Indian guides were present, standing in expectation. A light opens in the early evening sky. The sun's weak rays peer out, one last time, separating the clouds, but the ominous clouds move in to announce the evening.

Michelle walks forward towards the tree line where the woods began and ended with the prison walls. She turns ninety degrees and spots a storm door. She approaches it.

303

She opens the vial of holy water and sprinkles the ground ahead. She walk a few paces further towards the tree line and stops.

"Someone is here. Buried."
Then, as soon as Michelle articulated it, she is overwhelmed by perfume. Alice. "Alice. Are you here?" The scent of verbena.

Michelle approaches the storm door that leads to the basement. Through the basement's half-window she sees a man lying on a dirt floor. He is dressed in an old-fashioned farmers' overalls. The vision of him where he lay was going in and out like a television screen that wouldn't focus.
Michelle blinks. Realization dawns on her that she is seeing something from another time, another dimension: The vintage farmer's overalls, the tools on the wall and the horses' stalls. At one time, this was a stable.
Michelle strains to see in her mind's eye the identity of the man lying prone on the ground. She could not.
"I see a man!" The women rush to her side to look.

Suddenly, Michelle's legs sink about a foot, her calf halfway down with the ground. Jessica attempts to pull her mother up. Michelle points to the storm door. "Don't go there. I just saw a portal from another time."

The scent of verbena assails Michelle's senses. The sound of water, akin to a rolling river and a vision of a waterfall reaches her mind's eye. Someone was trying to connect with her with a pleasant thought. Angel Falls, her favorite spot came to mind.

"I'm here too, Michelle." A feminine voice she's heard before. It was in a dream and on an electronic voice recorder. However, this time she distinctly heard it with her own ears.

304

Michelle looks down at her feet. Her brace strains to keep her straight. Jake rushes and pulls his mother out with Jessica's help. "Someone's buried right beneath my feet. Someone get a shovel."

Walking around the house, Nancy and Pam survey the house's windows. Their eyes lock in unison at the basement's half-window, where they spot a form lying prone on the cement floor. "Someone's unconscious in there!" Nancy yells to Michelle. "You both see it?" Jessica nods. This time it was a woman.

Jake returns to his mother's side with a shovel and starts digging where Michelle points to the ground.

Michelle blinks and turns her attention back to the basement window, following the women's line of sight. It was a woman wearing modern clothing. She rushes to enter the storm door, but it slams shut. The women run to the front of the house. It was now seven thirty pm.

305

## Chapter Fifty Seven

### One hour ago

Julia touches the door, noting a vibration beyond. Something was still humming beyond the door. She wonders if it's the hot water heater, some equipment left to run and now needed repairs. She scans the entire door, searching for clues as it what it may have been used for. It didn't appear to be an exit to anywhere, but another room. A spare room of sorts, perhaps an area for storing tools which they already had in the separate garage where all the eerie events began. It looked similar in parts to a horse's stall, with hay here and there on the cement floor.

Anxious to exit the house in case Henry or some entity happened upon her, Julia raises her knife and pushes the wooden door in. The knob creaks as she turns it. Then, like a rusted tool awaiting a final reply, the knob comes off, rusted. It clangs onto the cement floor and a mouse scurries past. Julia jumps, her nerves on edge.

The door sways on its hinges. Immediately, she smells decay, putrefaction and death. Instinctively, she raises her arm to shield her nose from the inflammatory scent which makes her gag. The humming is more palpable now. It's not the clothes dryer, which carried the scent of dryer sheets, exotic in its lavender cleanness in the midst of dirt and mold. She turns back and the dryer isn't there.

The room was empty except for a few more wooden barrels and what appeared to be rows of bottles, still corked and unopened like wine. They lay on their sides in stacks, dusty, molded and covered in mouse droppings.

Julia searched for a light switch along the walls, wishing she had the fortitude to have brought a flashlight with her. She darts a look behind her to check. Convinced no one had entered the house, she enters the small room and approaches the barrel which appeared empty.

307

She spots a large candle, home made. Next to it, a flint. She strikes it several times against the barrel and then sees what appeared to be kindling. She sets to light a fire and then touches the candle wick. The weak flame illuminates part of the room. Musty, disused and very rustic.

Slowly, she approaches the barrel, aged with oaken sides, still intact. It seemed to shimmer, suggesting water inside. She peers.

The flame flickers and goes out as her face looks down into the barrel. The head of something floats. The water is deep red. Julia pauses to look up at the light between the slats of wood.
She turns back to peer in again…and backs away, finding her throat locked in a scream.

In the barrel, the head of a disembodied rat floats, eyes glassy and staring. Hairs from its ears poke out. Julia gasps and continues to back away. She trips. The place is infested with rats, she surmised with disgust.

Julia regains her balance, looks down to see where she had tripped and finds something huge prone on the floor. Something hums and another click - it's inside her head. All sounds of the night has suddenly vanished. It is quiet. Too quiet.

Suddenly, blood is all over the dirt floor and Julia is slipping. She had tripped on the body of a man in old-fashioned overalls. A farmer. His throat was slit and and he is holding a knife. He stares back at her as if frozen in accusation. He had Henry's face.

Henry. Dead on the ground. Julia tries to get away but she is sliding and slipping on Henry's blood.

Sliding and slipping.

308

Slipping.

Julia fights to get up as her jeans are now soaked in Henry's blood, his body just a few inches away, his head lolling to one side with only one tendon holding it in place.

Something flickers above her. At the next barrel, something appears to be making its way out. Hornets.
Hornets fly all over, covering the dusty bottles, Henry's body, Julia's hair and body.

Stings cover Julia as she struggles to get up from the slick blood, the knife in her hand slipping as she attempts to reach for the door and out. With all her might, she reaches the door, shuts it against the humming hornets. They were all over her hair.

Julia feels the first pangs of early labor, but it was only her second trimester. Then, blood spreads beneath her and she feels the room close in.

Laughter.

A few yards away, a man in silhouette stands with a large tree limb in hand. He had a fedora on and his eye gleamed red with hate.

Julia's vision darkens.

309

## Chapter Fifty Eight

## 1905

Alice rushes to the stables, Harry in pursuit. Her taffeta skirt catches on a nail protruding from a stall. Horses neigh as she struggles with the dress. She breathes heavily as she tugs, her effort causing her cheeks to turn red. She looks down at the cement floor and feels a gush between her legs. Her water broke.

Heavy with pregnancy, she tears the fabric, rushes to the stable door and runs outside. Leaves fly in the autumn air as she screams for help. Her screams remain unheard until a carriage thrums by, pulled by two horses. A man alights from the carriage and stands watching in surprise. He approaches.

Suddenly, Harry exits the house with a large stick. It appears as large as a tree trunk. He bolts for Alice, raises the stick as Alice raises her hands in a defensive posture. He pummels her, but the third blow, aimed at her head, is stalled. The man from the carriage intervenes, stopping Harry's arm in mid strike. He pulls Harry away and wrestles him to the ground. As the fracas resumes, a woman from the carriage rushes to Alice's side and ministers to her as a cart with a horse pulls up. Alice clambers onto the cart bruised and in labor.

The distinguished man aims a gun at Harry, but Harry manages to kick the man's hand, disengaging his gun. A farmer in overalls emerges from the stable alerted by horses that continue to neigh in fright. He dashes forward and grabs Harry, but Harry manages to wrestle him and slit the farmer's throat. The farmer dashes back into the stables, clutching his throat and falls dying into a stall. Harry dashes off into the adjacent field where the two men in pursuit lose sight of him.

At the hospital, nurses address Alice's wounds and help her as she goes into premature labor. Battered and bruised, she manages to deliver a stillborn child. Alice returns to her house alone, sent back to recover and mourn her lost infant. Unbeknownst to Alice, Harry is still at large, hiding in the woods near the prison. One night, Harry returns to the house and bludgeons her to death.

312

## **<u>Chapter Fifty Nine</u>**

At four and a half feet, they hit a shoe. It was a woman's boot. It was now nine pm. Small tell-tale pieces of fabric still clung to the skeleton, evidently dating back from the early nineteen hundreds. The clothing predated the house, the basement area apparently part of the original structure.

As the team stood by watching what Jake was steadily unraveling, Michelle and Nancy locate an axe in the garage. Nancy grabs the axe from the wall and dashes to the storm door. Wielding the axe over her head, Pam smashes through the bolt as Michelle descends the steps and enter the basement.

On the cement floor, Julia lies unconscious. Bruises and contusions were visible on her face and arms as if she had been battered. A knife lay nearby, clean and without blood. Michelle stands over Julia as Nancy attempts to resuscitate her. "Oh, please, wake up." Pam cries, inconsolable. Michelle touches Pam's shoulder in a gesture of support, as she speaks into her cell phone.
"The ambulance should be here any minute."
Julia coughs and regains consciousness. She looks at her sister's face and her pallor returns.

Michelle climbs the stone steps up to the area where Jake stood expectantly waiting with the rest of the team, clustered around the hole. Their faces mirror their disbelief and a sense of dread permeates the group. Michelle braced herself, wondering what or who she would find.

Michelle approaches, the rest of the team parting to allow her a view. As she approaches, the scent of verbena assails her nostrils, giving her pause. She was looking at a grave of a young woman, about Julia's age. Curly, dark hair was still connected to some parts of the skull; around the neck, a silver chain with a cross. On the sternum of the skeleton, untouched, was a brooch. The remains of a dress,

313

now in tatters and in advance stages of decay show it was a woman with a long dress from the turn of the century.

Jessica leans down, reaching for the brooch. It was a locket. She hands it to Michelle who opens it. Inside, still intact, but stained, was the sepia photograph of a young man. A striking resemblance to the prison photograph Michelle saw in a line up from the penitentiary archives shared by Ken LaMaster. The photo showed a younger man, but the eyes and jaw betrayed the identity of the man. It was none other than Harry, Alice's husband in life.

Michelle dials her cell again. "Please. Someone send the police as well." Michelle gazes down at the body of Alice. The scent of verbena, strong as ever. "We found you, Alice. We finally found you. It's over."

Suddenly, the sound of humming returns. Michelle turns to the storm door, now broken and yawing open to discover hundreds of hornets flying out into the sky. Julia's eyes open where she lies prone on the ground, awaiting an ambulance. "He's back. He's back. He's back!"

The sound of ambulance sirens permeate the neighborhood. Several people approach from the street, curious to see the emergency. They flee in the opposite direction once they see the swarm of hornets. The team flees back to their vehicles to seek shelter.
"It's just a ruse. They're not real." Michelle yells.
As fast as the hornets appeared, they all suddenly turned towards the woods and vanished.

Michelle watched as the insects vanished into the wood. "Go back where you came from, Harry. There is no place for you here."
Michelle returns to Julia's side as the ambulance pulls up. Two men, EMT's, emerge with a stretcher and place it on the ground where Julia now sits, sipping from a water bottle. One of the EMT's look down at Julia.

He reaches for her pulse and then inspects her face. "What's the matter with her? Was she bitten by the hornets?" He asks Pam. Pam examines her sister's arms and face in shock.

Julia looks down at herself as Michelle looks and searches Julia's face.

Where the bruises were, the arms were now clear. She no longer had bites from the hornets nor any contusions on her face or arms.

Julia looks up at Michelle. "What happened to Henry?"

315

316

# **Chapter Sixty**

## **The Final Act**

Henry sat by the coffee house window, watching the antique store across the street. He sips as he observes Julia exit the store and walk her way towards the car by the curb. On the storefront window, a hand reaches the "Open" sign and turns it to "Closed." He finishes his coffee and carelessly tosses it into the bin, missing it by inches. He passes an elderly woman on the way out, gruffly shouldering her as he rushes out of the shop.

Outside, the evening was brisk with the first signs of fall taking hold. His pace slackens as he pauses by his car. He lights a cigarette as he pulls the brim of his hat lower and eyes Julia turn the car engine on. He slides into his car and follows.

Down the street, Julia turns left onto the road leading to her house. Harry pauses, steps on the pedal and turns the car, keeping himself two car lengths behind to obscure himself from Julia. At the intersection, Henry eyes the penitentiary in the distance to his left. He follows and drives past Julia as she slides her car to the curb in front of the house they shared prior to the divorce.
He turns the car around and parks a street past the house under cover of trees. He exits in time to see a very pregnant Julia exit the car and approach.

On the front lawn, Henry observes the medium Michelle and three other women welcome Julia and take a basket from her. He recalls meeting Michelle as he watches. They proceed into the house. Henry crosses the street as he watches the women through the bay window of the lighted living room. Their hands linked, they appeared to be praying. He eyes the tree line and hastily jogs to the wood, entering it in a whoosh.

317

Within the wood, Henry lights a small fire and his eyes take on a faraway look. He sits and waits, but not long. He digs for a flashlight in his jacket and enters deeper into the wood, walking several yards in the fading light into the depths of the forest. Finally, Henry reaches his destination: The walls of the prison. He places his flashlight down on the ground as he squats and smokes, waiting. He looks up the prison's high walls, waiting and watching as he surveys the area. He glances at his watch and extinguishes his cigarette with the toe of his boot.

Inside the warm and inviting living room, Michelle prays the rosary with the investigative team as Julia prays silently with them. They stood in a circle with the coffee table in the center, a candle and a vial of holy water on the shiny cherrywood surface. Michelle opens her eyes as the team members rush to place monitors and other equipment for another night to detect any remaining spirits.
"Julia, we're here so that we can be sure you're safe. We want to make sure there's no other entities present that can harm you or your baby."
"I'm hoping whatever it is is now gone and Henry comes back to normal."
"I can only tell you that time will tell. Only God can guarantee it. "
"Was Henry possessed?"
"Henry had an attachment."
"That's why Alice made herself known to you?"
"I think so. She wanted her body found and also didn't want any more harm to come from Harry's vengeful spirit."
"How do we break this attachment from Henry?"
"I meant, we can only do what God allows us to do. Henry has to be willing."
"If he's not?"
"If he's not, we can't do anything about it."
Julia sighs in resignation. "I wish there was a way for the baby to know her father."
Nancy interjects. "I'm sure in time you can tell her about him."
"The good things." Jessica added.

318

"Let's begin." Michelle leads the group towards the stairs. "We'll start at the top with our devices, then work our way down. We'll pray and bless every room where we detect harmful entities. We help cross over the good ones if there's any. Okay?"
"Yes, okay."
"The basement we'll cleanse and then the outside into the garage."
"The garage." Julia mused.
"Yes. We'll save that for last."
"Okay."


Henry stands expectantly as he sees something in the darkness of the vast prison wall slither down towards him. A formless smoke, taking shape as it slithers down the wall of the penitentiary. He shuts his eyes and opens them again in disbelief. Then, the form gains a visage. A reptilian face with slit eyes like a snake's. Henry gasps. He backs away as the tendons and sinew reach out to him, a gigantic human reptile with fangs. His mind must be playing tricks on him, Henry surmised. However, it was too real.
It looked like an insect or reptile he'd seen in a movie. His favorite movie.
Then, one tentacle with reptilian scales reaches out.
That was enough.
Henry bolts, his adrenaline taking over.

Henry runs through the wood, but as the clearing towards his property gets closer, he hears an unmistakable 'click'.
Something shifts inside Henry. He senses a reeling feeling as if he's about to faint, but continues to run.

Suddenly, the tree line and clearing were no longer there.
Henry finds himself in a field of tall grass. He lifts his boots to find they are soaked in mud and weeds. He turns to look back and sees the specter with snake

319

eyes skimming the surface of the field from the woods. It began to look like the creature in the movie, "Alien."

Henry stares at the specter two times taller than him as it approaches with stealth, silently skimming the surface of the field as if it was floating.
It seems to be floating, Henry figures in his head. How could that be?

He looks down at his feet.
"How the fuck did I get here?" Henry announces to no one. He eyes his house in the distance with the warmth of the lights glowing through the familiar windows. He craves for the house that was his home.
He steps towards the house, away from the penitentiary and the field, but his feet sink deeper.
"What…". He looks up and finds the specter is gaining ground.
Closer.
Closer.
A hum.
Humming.
"What the heck is going…".
Henry pulls at his legs. He is steadfastly stuck. He pulls with effort and is doggedly moving, one foot and then another in slow progress.
Henry begins to sweat. "Someone help me!"
He sees the lighted windows of the house, the women who appear to be eating dinner. His house. A dinner he would want, would be eating with Julia if he had still been there. He finds he is starving, sweaty and very nervous.

Yards away, above the field, the security lights come on around the penitentiary. It illuminates the surrounding field around him in time for him to see his own legs up to the knees in tall grass.
He struggles to pull one foot up, one step, and then the other foot, attempting to free it.

320

Then before he knew it, he could feel the vibration and the humming issuing from the specter. It was weaving in and out like a television out of focus, like it was losing the internet on a podcast.
Frozen, then moving and skimming the field... frozen, then moving... closer... closer.
The serpent, the reptilian creature, was so dark and nebulous, it was drowning out the light.
Henry found himself shrouded in darkness, unable to see except for the specter. Closing in.
Henry struggles with all his might.
One foot free.
Next foot.
Closer.

Henry screams as his feet sink deeper into the mire.
He reaches up to the sky, but only the mouth of the specter meets him.
Fangs.

Michelle's eyes pop open as she makes eye contact with something in the distance - through the dining room window and into the field beyond the next house.
Almost done with their late dinner, hosted by Julia, Michelle bolts up from her chair as she sees someone being pursued. The women pause from their talk. Right past the neighbor's stucco home, in the field where the prison guards patrol when an inmate escapes, she sees someone struggling away. He or she was pursued by something shapeshifting. Then, she saw two prison guards, their flashlights aimed in the same direction.
He appeared lost, stuck and wandering as she was, months and months ago before she learned how deluding evil can be. A huge shapeshifter in the middle of the field was in pursuit.
It looked like the creature in the movie, 'Alien.'

321

"What is it, Michelle?" Pam follows Michelle's line of sight.
"You see what's chasing the man?"
"The guards?" Julia asks.
"Prison guards." Jessica qualifies.
"No, there's something between them."

Only Michelle could see it. Only Michelle and the man struggling to get away.

322

## Chapter Sixty One

The tower guard, young and eager in his crisp uniform, spots a man making his way doggedly into the field around nine-thirty pm. He records it on the log and notes the man's clothing, including his boots. He hits a round green button on his console and two additional tower lights come on. He trains the spotlights on the man. He follows the man with his eyes through the glass windows of the tower: The figure stumbles his way through the kudzu of the swampy terrain. The guard, unsure, attempts to assure himself it wasn't an inmate who had escaped. The clothing wasn't the standard bright orange which reminded him of the overalls that his father used to wear when he was a large equipment mechanic. However, on second thought, the man seemed desperate to escape something, as if something was pursuing him.

As he watches, he picks up the black phone, calls it into the dispatch room and to get the cameras trained on the man. No sense letting it go just in case a prisoner managed to steal some civilian clothing, stashed from some recent visitor who handed it to him. It would have been his job to call it in anyway, so he did.

As the guard follows with his eyes, he trains his gun with the scope on the back of the man's figure, aiming it just in case he got a call it was an inmate. He had tranquilizer darts on as he would not want to inflict a mortal wound and lose his job. Another guard goes out, on patrol. The tower guard spots the familiar uniform as the guard exits from somewhere below and walks the field, joined by a third guard. He is now glad he called it in.

They quickly gain on the man who now appears to be screaming. More likely, the man was yelling profanities at the guards, but it was more the scream of one mortally in peril. As they close in, the man cowers and wrestles with them as if he

324

was fighting for his life. They attempt to calm him, secure him and the tower guard sees the man's face from his vantage: Terror. The man was in terror.

Suddenly, as fast as the man had appeared, he vanishes. The tower guard scratches his head as he unwraps a Butterfinger bar, as if it was a movie. He recalls a scene where Tom Cruise was running as fast as this man with his daughter in a sci fi film, but he forgets the title. He watches his colleagues, the guards, standing stupefied, searching and surveying the area for the man. He sees them call into their walkie talkies as his own comes to life.
"He just up and disappeared somewhere."
"Say that again, Jim?"
"We can't find him."
"Look around. He dove into the grass, maybe. What the shit."
"Tower one and two, stay frosty. He's down there."

The man had vanished into thin air.

It was eleven pm by the time the paranormal team had completed their task of cleansing and blessing Julia and Henry's home from top to bottom. As planned, they saved the garage for last, pulling the plug off the electrical socket from the flat-screen TV as the team prayed and Michelle sprinkled salt and holy water on all four sides of the structure. As Jake walked away from the television set, it came back on, showing a scene from the Alien movie. Sigourney Weaver, shooting a laser gun, blasting the creature as she held on to a small child.

Suddenly, it came to Michelle. The shapeshifter in the field just hours ago.

The team stops in their tracks, wondering and amazed as Michelle approaches the electrical device. She checked the plug again to the television. Disconnected. Then, finally, the television winked out as the creature falls into space, out of the hatch. Julia stands near Michelle with a questioning look. "Did it work?"

325

"Give it time."

By the time they exited to their vehicles, it was midnight. At one in the morning, Julia, now alone in the house, was awaken by a loud rapping on the front door.

Julia turns the porch lights on, now fixed and bright. She wraps a dressing gown about her as she turns each light on from the stairs and into the living room. The house was warm, inviting and cheerful for a change. She opens the front door to discover two uniformed policemen standing there, flashing their badges. They were apologetic, aware of the lateness of the hour, but they had an urgent message for Julia.

In the bedroom Michelle shares with her husband, a phone rings by her bedside. Michelle's eyes were open, awake as she processes the events of the night, hoping she did what she had to do with perfection: Protective rituals before entering the site, praying fervently with faith and exiting after a circle of protection had been instilled. Her circle of family and friends that made up her team amplified her faith. Their connectedness as a paranormal community ratcheted the positive energy they needed to break the entity.

Like Superman, a thought jumped out at Michelle, inspired by things unseen around her: kryptonite. The weakness of the entity who was Harry in life had been subdued by the three important things: Protection from Saint Micheal, faith and finally the willingness of an entire team to push belief to the limit. The entity's kryptonite. She felt the support and presence of not only Alice, but Paul, Clementine and someone close to her. Someone who loved her in life. She resolves that night to visit Angel Falls, the place of solace for her and her days of hiking with her oldest brother, Rob.

As she reaches for the phone, Michelle glances at the ceiling fan and remembers the serpent she had seen before, a large reptile which uncoiled itself in her dream. Nothing there. The fan was just a fan, reflecting some light from the bedroom

326

window. Michelle picks up the phone as David rouses from sleep and reminds her she needed to return the following night to the slaves' house. She had to cross over the stranded souls who starved to death in life. Get some sleep, David said, they're not going anywhere. Michelle had still to complete the investigation there that had been interrupted by Julia's referral, but she had an important appointment to have her back brace removed.

Sleep, then the appointment, and later the investigation follow up on the Missouri slaves' house.

Julia's voice on the phone was real. Michelle listens, enrapt.

Henry had been found. His body, waterlogged and without boots was found on the field, his eyes in a state of shock. He had suffocated. At the coroner's office, they found hornets inside his mouth and his nose. How they got there, no one knows. Inside Henry's pocket were his car keys and a keychain. The keychain had a plastic creature: The alien from the Alien movie.

327

## Chapter Sixty Two

## The House of Fear

The brick and stucco house stood out in the small rural neighborhood because of its aura of loneliness and decay. Just a few yards away, almost as one would expect, an old pre-civil war cemetery stood, the mausoleum of one prominent family dominating the small lot. Composed of marble and with a stone roof, the mausoleum was that of a slaveowner, a man who constructed the adjacent house of brick and stucco from slaves' hands. The slaveowner, wealthy for his time, moved his family of five into the home and kept the slaves who help build it to maintain and work for the home.

Although the house dated back to pre-civil war days, the interior could still exude a quiet elegance if it were to be renovated. The lush Persian carpet still dominates the entry foyer, the crystals from the chandelier, now dusty and dull, could still be polished one by one if time and loving hands were invested upon it.

During its time of splendor, adjacent to the house on two sides, left and back, a plantation of corn and tobacco can be seen as far as the eye can see. Wrapped in this cocoon between the plantation and the cemetery to the right, the house could only be seen from the front via a winding pebbled path that led up to the handsome columns of the deep and shady porch. The property comprised of fifty acres which included the family cemetery to the right and the plantation to the left and back.

After the civil war, the house went through a succession of owners after the original landowner passed. The original landowner's finances dwindled when his land became fallow, the blood of soldiers cursing his fields. His loyal servants, indentured slaves prior to the civil war, were left to fend for themselves, all seven, when the last family member of the landowner chose to leave the plantation at the end of the civil war in 1865. Poor, destitute, unable to engage in commerce to sustain the land and with little education, the slaves ate off what they could from whatever harvest remained. However the land remained fallow and they reportedly starved to death.

The house remained empty for a number of years after the civil war, then a succession of owners found the house through the government. It was abandoned again by nineteen thirty and remained in a state of what would be considered condemned, the adjacent field previously used for corn and other grain now yielding to a forest. Children and teens would stumble upon the house through the forest and circle it, their parents forbidding them to enter or loiter about. Until one late afternoon in December of twenty-nineteen, a family of four moved into the home and the father, a businessman, decided to restore the house.

A rare find in this area of Missouri, the businessman planned to restore it to its former splendor. By standards, the house was not as large nor opulent as other mansions. It could only be called a house since it only had eight bedrooms, one dining room and a large kitchen which had several small clapboard bedrooms for the slaves who served there. The privacy afforded by the enveloping forest made it attractive, despite it's proximity to a cemetery in ruin. The home was now only a few acres, the cemetery considered an interesting historical artifact. The aura of disuse and gloom did not discourage the new owner, young and energetic as he is. He saw an opportunity to restore a historic home replete with a cemetery. He didn't mind its reputation nor the tall grass that began to edge its way into the back where the clapboard rooms of slaves ended. It was a bargain.

Despite its modest size, the family who originally owned it had slaves who lived in the house. A black woman and her two daughters lived within the servants' quarters which were small, threadbare and poorly lit rooms nestled behind the kitchen and under the main staircase. The new owner decided he would use the small rooms in the back of the house as storage and a pantry of sorts for his growing family. He would hook up electricity and heat the rooms, adding double walls and insulation once the summer began in earnest.

330

Thus it came to pass that while sections of the house were repainted, brought up to 'code' by building inspectors, the new woman of the house moved in with her children and all was quiet for a while as the winter of twenty twenty ended. The family had not even began the major renovations to the house as the snowy weather forbade any type of outdoor construction or painting. The house remained in its sorry state, the front porch fallen in places, the paint around the aged windows peeling. It was during one evening as the family sat down for dinner that they had their first encounter with the former residents of the house. It was now the beginning of March and the pandemic of twenty-twenty was about to imprison them in a strange house.

While Michelle restlessly awaited the brace to be removed from her back, she received a call while sunning herself in the backyard of her home. Fall's leaves cascaded down her yard in earnest, the wind taking a turn, but that one day had one sudden sun. It was the day when she felt more energetic despite the lingering pain of the stitches, the itching that preceded the healing, that her landline rang. Still awaiting the final result of the extensive clearing and cleansing of Julia's house, Michelle would embark on her next challenging case, a home riddled by spirits who banged on walls, yelled profanities and turned furniture upside down and tossed clothing through windows in the middle of the night.

The feminine voice at the other end of the line told Michelle that they were desperate to be rid of the noises in the home and were in the process of 'ruling out' vermin as the cause of the noise. A few weeks later, while Julia mourned her husband's tragic death under terrifying circumstances, Michelle received another call, this time from the husband, the businessman.
Vermin had been ruled out. Tim, stoic and sounding professional on the phone appeared reserved, but his voice betrayed his desperation. The inspection by a pest control service yielded no conclusion, but a baffling discovery: In the small bedrooms still intact and tucked behind the kitchen were old moth-eaten clothing,

331

in the style of the previous century, neatly folded and stacked inside a small cabinet. Clothing faded and now in tatters, they appeared to be remnants of a life of slavery. Tools were found scattered in a nearby shed, dating back centuries old.

As the pest control crew entered the other bedrooms in search of mice, they also found the skull of a small child. Michelle shivers and sighs involuntarily. While the man recites several strange incidents, Michelle reaches for her file and pen. This home warranted an investigation and most likely, a cleansing and clearing of spirits. She had to return immediately as soon as the pandemic allowed her.

332

## Chapter Sixty Three

## Crossing Over

The team stepped out of the white SUV, their equipment stowed and ready in the compartment. The house stood silently, expectant like a beast awaiting to pounce. The surrounding wood encroached on the sides of the property, as if ready to take over. The front porch, however, stood open and it appeared to have been recently painted and free of debris. The front door, still unpainted, stood slightly open as if in invitation. In places, mold still caked on one side of the gutter and the scent of pine and aging still made the edifice appear from a forgotten time. Until now.

Michelle took her sneakers off despite the chill of the weather, her feet surrounded immediately by grass and sodden leaves. Nancy approached and removed her sneakers as well, then Jessica and Jake. Now barefooted, they linked hands and stood in a circle and recited the Lord's prayer, then the Saint Micheal prayer of protection. Michelle silently ended the circle by nodding to the next and then the next, checking in that all were ready.
They all sat and laced their sneakers, returned to the car and proceeded to carry the paranormal equipment into the house one by one.

The lights came on as the team members dispersed to place the equipment at strategic points within the house. In the hall, Michelle walked up to the foyer table and hung a rosary around a bust. Vials of holy water were dispersed among the members as they scanned the house, looking into the adjacent rooms. Michelle turns on the ghost box for electronic voice phenomena (EVP), the rem pod, K2 Meter and cat balls in succession. Jessica takes the cat balls, placing them down the hall, across from the dining area and at the entrance to the living room.

The equipment was now all over the first floor of the house. Immediately, the rem pod and K2 meter went to flashing red in the living room. Both equipments signals to the team that there was a spirit very close to them. It is present.

"Whoever is in here, we are here to see what you need." Michelle intoned into the room.
"We want to communicate with you." Jessica followed.
"We want to see who you are." Nancy spoke to no one in particular.

Jake shuts all the lights, plummeting the team in darkness. The K2 meter and the rem pod continues to cast bright red glows all over the crew, their faces enrapt. Jake flicks on a flashlight as he powers on the spirit talker app on his cellphone, and finally, the SLS camera. A hand-held voice recorder sits on the mantelpiece. Nancy grabs it and stands expectantly as Michelle signals her to walk towards the living room. Jake follows, holding the cellphone ahead of him.

A squeak issues from the Paranormal Music equipment. Michelle turns and watches cat balls light up from three corners of the vast hallway. "Look", she whispers. Jessica turns, then Nancy. The balls were rolling towards Michelle.

The SLS camera captures the outline of a spirit. It is moving towards them from the dining room, its jerky outlined movements almost like a cartoon. "Check the living room." Michelle tells Jake.
Jake turns the camera and the living room shows a smaller figure as it stands near the mantelpiece.

Down the hall towards the kitchens, steps issue from somewhere above them. A hollow sound evinces from the ghost box. Michelle eyes the SLS camera, catching the energy outline of two spirits near them in the living room.

"How many of you are here?"
The SLS camera shows three figures outlined.

335

"Three." The EVP squeaks.
"Say again."
"Three."
Michelle closes her eyes.
A familiar scent. Verbena. Then, Lily of the Valley. Both Alice and Mary Michelle were there.
"Alice and Mary Michelle. If you're here, please let me know."
A red light flashes from the rem pod. All three cat balls go green.
"Thank you for being here. Is there anyone else?"
"The ones that live in this house. Come forward." Jessica adds.

The paranormal music box evinces a squeaky tone and then a voice. "We're three."
"Old, young?"
"Me and my two children."
"What do you want from us?"
"Free us."

Michelle knew what she had to do.
"We're going to pray now. Will you pray with us?"

All equipment goes berserk. All lights turn from green to bright red, the recorder screams "Yes."
"Yes." From the paranormal music box.
"Please."

Jake looks on in awe. The SLS camera shows three figures moving towards Michelle: One tall spirit, two smaller ones.
"Michelle, help them." It was Mary Michelle. This time she felt the breath by her ear.

"Let's pray together in faith." Michelle announces as they link hands in the living room.

337

338

# **Chapter Sixty Four**

## **Night**


David sips, then his face turns sour. He pours it down the sink. On the way out of the kitchen, he spies a tin and opens it. Oatmeal cookies. David reaches in like a child, bites through, but he suddenly pulls his foot away in fright. The long haired brown and white cat was brushing against his leg, her eyes luminous and flecked with worry like his. David sighs in relief. He had been jittery lately.

"Kelly. What's the matter, baby girl?"
He chews and picks up the cat with one arm as he saunters up the steps back to the bedroom. In the deep recesses of his mind, David wonders whether he was projecting his own worries on the cat. She purred as he carried her towards the bedroom, but then he notes her hairs stand on end.

He pauses. He thought he heard wings flapping behind the closed door. Large wings like that of an albatross. Perhaps more like an eagle, David ponders, as he is in Kansas. Suddenly the cat leaps and darts back down the stairs.
Behind him, another bedroom door opens down the hall. Jake, a study in pajamas stare back, sleep still in his eyes.
"Did you hear that, Dad?" He whispers.

Wings flap, then an impenetrable silence. A female moan.
"It's Mom." Jake offers and darts for the master bedroom past his father.
Dave turns the knob to their room as Jake joins him.

In the half-light of the sheer curtains, David sees something clutching the edge of the wooden floorboard of the large bed. It intently stares down at Michelle who lay uneasily turning under the sheets as if in the throes of a nightmare, her eyes shut as she continued an internal struggle. She moaned. David approached and the

339

creature turned to eye him. It had the visage of a human, but with the outline of a bat. David's head screamed in terror, but his lips failed. A palpable sense of menace and hate assailed them.

David finally let out a gasp as Jake held up a stick of sorts.

The creature eyes Jake and unfolded its wings in reply. Dave backed away, stunned at its sheer size.

"Get out!" Jake yelled as he approached, both hands in a viselike grip around a metal stick. David stared in shock at his son and realized he was holding his prized golf putter. Slowly, he looked back to where his son focused his eyes and discovers a growling visage of hate.

The creature opened its mouth, eyes red. Then it turned and flew through the closed glass of the window.
The men stood speechless and then bolted down the stairs in pursuit.

Michelle sat up from the bed. Too fast. She saw stars as her heart pounded. Her back shot in a paroxysm of pain, reminding her of the stitches that still pulled when she made a sudden move.
Footsteps. Yelling. She heard her husband's voice and then her son's, as the front door sprung open below. She senses malice in the aftermath, a cloying scent of animal dung and a fear grips her as she reaches for the edge of the bed.

Michelle gingerly steps onto the carpeted floor and approaches the window, pulling it up. She grimaced with effort.

Her husband and son were on the front walk, surveying the road and the surrounding neighborhood. Searching, it seemed. David looked up and they locked eyes.

340

"Come back. Please." Michelle yells from the window. She turns and feels something stare her down, but there was nothing there. Michelle knew it was gone, but out of habit, she approaches the closet. Opening the closet door, she inspects the clothes in their hangers. She moves each one methodically and then looks up at the shoeboxes.

She takes one box out and opens it. A metal cross. A vial of holy water labeled "Medjugorje." She takes it out and begins to intone a prayer, closing her eyes. A hand touches and stays, the warmth penetrating her shoulder. It was David.

"You're okay?" He asked with uncertainty. Behind him stood Jake, eyes wary, still holding the putter. "Mom, didn't you see something like that when you were a teenager?"

"Yes, like a Mothman. Glad you woke me. It was, I thought, in my dreams."
"Is it back?"
"I hope not."
"I'll keep the lights on and stay up a bit until you sleep, honey." David offered.
Jake makes for the hallway, retiring for the night. "Yell if you need me, Dad."
"I think it's gone… for now. Go to bed, son. Glad you're staying with us."
"Okay, Mom?"
"Thank you. I am." Michelle replies. She turns and looks at the closet and is lost in a distant memory. The closet is deep and dark as Michelle ponders and recalls a childhood room.

A click. The room shifts.
Michelle now knows she's entering a portal.

It's time to confront the hat man. She's ready.

341

## Chapter Sixty Five

## Angel Falls

On the edge of a forest, Michelle parks her car. She emerges alone, the sun behind her. It is half past eleven in the morning. Her cotton sundress flows freely behind her, blown in waves by a gentle breeze, her hair loose behind her back. With bare arms, she raises her hands to the air as her bare toes touch the earth.

She is free. Liberated from her back brace, Michelle approaches with her sandals in one hand, one rosary in the other. She pauses at the tree line and takes the path less frequently walked as she enters the forest. The canopy of trees soon envelope her as her dress in hues of blue and pink are soon engulfed by the restive foliage.

Michelle comes to a rocky ledge and approaches a copse of trees on a hill. Under them, a large flat rock welcomes her. She sits. Ahead, the gush of flowing water drown out the birdsong and the steady stream ahead. A waterfall, grand and silver in the sun, cascade down into a stream and into the river.

Michelle grasps her rosary, inhaling in as the waterfall lulls her into a land of enchantment. Melodic in its rhythm and flow, she is soon caught in the chant of the beads she grasps in an anthem to a God who has stayed by her side. The sun reaches its zenith, casting a direct glow amplified by the waterfall onto Michelle. Behind her and around her, trees reach up to the light and the land has no shadows.

Michelle feels the gentle whisper of the breeze and detects the visage of a young man, his life cut short by endless pain. She feels his gentle kindness, the love radiating and radiated back by her angels. On the promontory above the waterfall, she sees a light glimmer, taking shape, renewing its energy with vigor. She shuts her eyes in a gesture of thanks for this presence and the brother who had been there

for her in her darkest hour. Then, she opens her eyes to the light... and a feeling of flying assails her, a feeling of buoyancy and endless possibility.
Within the leaves of trees, it departs and takes flight: A white dove soaring limitless into a vast sky. It glows one final time, flapping its wings of white over and past Michelle. She follows with her eyes uplifted until it is lost into the firmament of day.

The light had radiated and shined on Michelle as it did long ago in the little playground, in the little school, while Michelle awaited her mother.
She remembers.

Not so long ago, on a playground, with the school monitor: The light from the tree - and the lady who came and cast a ray of light on her, beckoning and asking Michelle not to be afraid.

Michelle is no longer afraid.

344

## Post Script

## The Hat Man

Out of the depths of social media is a phenomena that has reached a wide mainstream audience of paranormal followers. It has recently in the last decade taken hold of authors of the paranormal and producers of true horror films. Reports of regular people encountering an apparition coined "The Hat Man" has joined the ranks of Slender man which came out of a young man's post on the forum, Creepypasta; to Black-Eyed Kids seen worldwide in remote villages and small far-off enclaves of sleepy towns; to sightings of the Rake, a creature that appears alien in origin. Like its predecessors, the hat man sightings appear to the hapless and unsuspecting, arresting them when they're the most vulnerable: When they're alone.

However, unlike the rake, slender man or black-eyed kids, which is usually seen out in the forests, the fields and in lonely lanes and roads, the hat man tends to be seen INSIDE a dwelling. These specters are usually seen outside windows, inside buildings and in homes.

As intimate as inside a person's bedroom.

Within the penitentiary walls of the Lansing Correctional Facility, Michelle and her daughter Jessica toured the prison and encountered numerous entities in the company of a small tour group. Some of the group's members dispersed after several terrifying experiences while on the tour, including being hailed by stones and hearing disembodied voices as they walked the halls of the prison's old section. Jessica herself recalls an entity in the psychiatric wing which she would not recount nor was willing to revisit. Michelle was scratched and clawed.

346

Despite the encounters, Michelle chose with Jessica to remain on the tour with a few others, including a woman whose Jewish faith provoked a Neo-Nazi entity. As Michelle entered an area called the 'dungeon', she encountered and chose to cross over a soul whose spirit was tormented by a Neo-Nazi entity in life. Freeing the spirit, Michelle further catalyzed the horror: The Neo-Nazi entity was in the cell with her.

It was during that visit that the same entity may have ventured out of the building and attached itself to Michelle, seeing her as a challenge after witnessing her strong desire to free souls from what Roman Catholicism would term Purgatory - the realm reserved for those who had sinned and remained outside the gates of heaven.

Subsequent encounters of a serpent-like creature, a reptilian, and finally a man with a fedora style hat has been sighted and experienced by Michelle. The subsequent health issues she is in recovery from at the time of this writing may have been due to her involvement in the rescue and crossing over of souls. Such is the risk for the very few whose purity of intention is to seek freedom for stranded souls so they may cross to the Light of God.

To learn more about the Hat Man and related phenomena:

Google or Amazon:
D.W. Pasulka
Heidi Hollis
David Weatherly

To learn about the concept of reincarnation and karma:

Google or Amazon:
Brian Weiss
Michael Newton
Dolores Cannon

Laura Lynn Jackson
John Burke

To learn the history of the Leavenworth prison of Kansas:

On Amazon:
Kenneth M. LaMaster

348

349

# <u>Appendix:</u>

The following Roman Catholic prayers are used in the rituals of protection and cleansing.

**Prayer to Saint Micheal, The Archangel -**

Saint Michael the Archangel, defend us in battle. Be our protection against the wickedness and snares of the devil; May God rebuke him, we humbly pray; And do thou, O Prince of the Heavenly Host, by the power of God, thrust into hell Satan and all evil spirits who wander through the world for the ruin of souls. Amen.

**Prayer Against Evil -**

Spirit of our God, Father, Son and Holy Spirit, Most Holy Trinity, descend upon me. Please purify me, mold me, fill me with yourself and use me. Banish all the forces of evil from me; destroy them, vanquish them so that I can be healthy and do good deeds.

Banish from me all curses, hexes, spells, witchcraft, black magic, demonic assignments, malefic and the evil eye; diabolic infestations, oppressions, possessions; all that is evil and sinful; jealousy, treachery, envy; all physical, psychological, moral spiritual and diabolical ailments; as well as all enticing spirits, deaf, dumb, blind, mute and sleeping spirits, new-age spirits, occult spirits, religious spirits, antichrist spirits and any other spirits of death and darkness.

I command and bid all the powers who molest me - by the power of God Almighty, in the name of Jesus Christ my Savior - to leave me forever, and to be consigned into the everlasting lake of fire, that they may never again touch me or any other creature in the entire world. Amen.

### Binding Evil Spirits -

In the name of the Lord Jesus Christ of Nazareth, I stand with the power of the Lord God Almighty to bind Satan and all his evil spirits, demonic forces, satanic powers, principalities, along with all kings and princes of terrors, from the air, water, fire, ground, netherworld, and the evil forces of nature.

I take authority over all demonic assignments and functions of destruction sent against me and I expose all demonic forces as weakened, defeated enemies of Jesus Christ. I stand with the power of the Lord God Almighty to bind all enemies of Christ present together, all demonic entities under their one and highest authority, and I command these spirits into the abyss to never again return.

I arise today with the power of the Lord God Almighty to call forth the heavenly host, the holy angels of God, to surround and protect, and cleanse with God's holy light all areas vacated by the forces of evil. I ask the Holy Spirit to permeate my mind, heart, body, soul and spirit, creating a hunger and thirst for God's holy Word, and to fill me with the life and love of my Lord, Jesus Christ.

### Closing of Deliverance Prayers -

Thank you, Lord Jesus, for awakening my sleeping spirit and bringing me into your light. Thank you, Lord, for transforming me by the renewing of my mind. Thank you, Lord, for pouring out your Spirit on me, and revealing your Word to me. Thank you, Lord, for giving your angels charge over me in all my ways. Thank you for my faith in you and that from my innermost being shall flow rivers of living water. Thank you for directing my mind and heart into the love of the

351

Father and the steadfastness of all Your ways. Fill me to overflowing with your life and love, my Lord and King, Jesus Christ.

For further prayers, please refer to the prayers of Saint Pio of Pietrelcina at:
Capuchin Franciscan Friars
P.O. Box 839
Union City, NJ 07087    (201) 863-4036  Or the website:  https://
www.padrepiodevotions.org

## Conclusion

Michelle's discovery as a teenager of her abilities which began at the tender age of five changed the course of her life and distinguished her from the rest. Her mother, her daughter Jessica and her two brothers, Rob and Ron in lesser degrees share this same gift of second sight.

Michelle is unique in her ability to cross over souls compared to the rest of her family. Since her tour of the prison where she began to feel less threatened by her ability to reach and assist souls stranded on earth, Michelle has helped over one hundred souls to cross over to the light. Despite the psychic and physical attacks she repeatedly suffered in the hands of lesser spirits or dark entities who sought to stop her, Michelle continues to thrive. Since her operation to ameliorate her back which was left unexplained as to the cause, Michelle has received over twenty case referrals to investigate at the time of this writing.

Rob Lemke, her brother in life, continues to make his presence felt and continues to protect from beyond the grave. Alice remains in Michelle's home and Michelle feels Alice may be the adult human version of Mary Michelle, her guardian angel.

If you need help in your home or place of business and feel you need a paranormal investigation, you may reach the real Michelle Lemke-Budke of First City Paranormal of Kansas by contacting her by email, by phone or Facebook messenger:

Michelle Lemke-Budke
michellebudke@aol.com
(913) 306-4959
Messenger App: Michelle Lemke-Budke

All cases are strictly confidential.

353

Michelle, age sixteen. High School photo.

The Lemke Family. Left to right: Rob, Ron, Michelle, Charlene and Larry Lemke.
Circa 1972.

## Current Members of First City Paranormal of Kansas

The following in alphabetical order are the real member investigators of Michelle Lemke-Budke's paranormal team as of the publication of this book:

Cheryl Budke
Jake Budke
Jessica Budke
Toni Cox
Nancy Gann
Vicki Kosman
Sue Lednicky
Brenda Lemke
Rich Lemke

Michelle Budke extends her heartfelt thanks to the entire team for their participation and willingness to take part in her circle of Light. Together with Michelle, they amplify the gift of spiritual healing to all souls who seek ascension into heaven.

*"There comes that time when the soul must once again leave the sanctuary of the spirit world for another trip to earth. This decision is not an easy one. Souls must prepare to leave the world of total wisdom, where they exist in a blissful state of freedom, for the physical and mental demands of a physical body."*
*- Dr. Michael Newton, "Journey of Souls".*

If you loved this book, please kindly consider giving me a review on Amazon or Goodreads. A strong rating and a few words of how you felt about the book goes a long way for authors like me who began our creative endeavor at the close of their formal career.

Follow me on Facebook @AnnaMariaManalo - Author or @TheSinisterArchives on Instagram and TikTok.

Have a story to tell? Contribute to my blog by emailing me at cinescriber@gmail.com

Website for updates on new releases? Blog of true encounters with eerie and horrifying beings?

Check out https://www.annamariamanaloauthor.com

Thank you for purchasing this book.

## SOON THIS SPRING OF 2025:

### **The Shopkeeper of Salerno**

A novel based on a true account of two tourists who unfortunately stayed overnight at a shopkeeper's home after missing their tour bus. What followed them back to the UK will reveal the depravity of the Nazi occupation of Italy in World War II.

BONUS CHAPTERS:   A Sneak Peek -


## The Shopkeeper of Salerno
## A supernatural suspense novel based on a true story from WWII


### Chapter 1


Alleghria pushes the wet mop on the terracotta floor, shiny and worn from centuries of use. She notes another tourist bus, exhaust issuing from its tailpipe, had just stopped in front of the square several yards ahead. As its brakes screech to a halt, a line of passengers descend in a medley of chatter. Voices with colorful accents, some foreign, some familiar, reach her ears as a group approaches their area of shops. Local shopkeepers, women dressed like her in a dress or men in jeans sipping drinks like her husband Iver, paused to watch. She senses the usual excitement that unfolds with every tour bus.

Businessmen in tailored summer suits, women garbed in all fashions from expensive Milan-cut dresses to young girls in shorts that showed too much, were sidestepping the tourists as they hurried about their normal day to return to work or play. Like the groups before them that poured into her shop earlier that Tuesday, the tourists appeared bewildered, if not in awe as they trod on the cobblestones from the bus and found their way to the curb. Forty or so of them, she counted, out of place in manner and dress in the late afternoon of a hot July day in Salerno. Polyester did not suit the Italian weather.

Among the cohort of tourists, exhausted and weary-looking, is a woman with her thick brown hair peering from a wide-brimmed hat, her wrinkled cotton dress exuding red poppies on a green background. She appears alive and curious, less weary like the man with a shock of blond hair in bermuda shorts who watches his step next to her. His shirt appeared to be crumpled, but new, the newness even speaking "expensive" as the cut was impeccably tailored, perhaps European-made. The couple in their early thirties joined the throng of tourists who appeared disoriented, if not lost. They pause at the central fountain, watching the rotational cascade of water to take in a photograph.

The man's light eyes appeared cautious but with an air of reserve, one arm protectively around the woman, obviously sweating in reply to the mid-July heat. His light-colored short pants reminded Allegrhia of the nineteen twenties when men were dressed to impress and flaunt their masculinity. However, as the couple paused just a few feet from her, the short-sleeved shirt made of linen seemed stuck to his back as he turned away from Allegrhia and offered a bottle of water to the woman. The woman pushed her dark hair further into the hat and sipped with efficiency, but with a certain daintiness. She whirled around to survey her surroundings and locked eyes with Alleghria.

Alleghria made a fleeting movement to shield her eyes from the young woman who studied her, then her shop beyond. She sensed the woman's interest in her shop as it was large and well-appointed with a heady and attractive array of confections: Baci, Perugina, Cote-D'or from France and even Polish chocolates

361

from Krakow. However, Allegrhia was a demure type and proud. She didn't want to look overly eager to sell to the group nor appear desperate to meet the day's profits. Behind her lay the panoply of marzipan, or almond paste: in fruit shapes, animal shapes and those enrobed in a dark chocolate shell, handmade by artisans in places Allegria herself had not visited. Those were one of her top sellers and always drew the eyes of the tourists from overseas. However, Iver had visited as Iver, her Norseman husband of twenty two years, was her buyer of goods.

Whereas Allegrhia preferred to stay close to home and tend to the needs of her elderly aunt Ariana, Iver loved perusing the goods that would later garnish the front windows of the shop. He would fly to the UK, take the fast trains up to Ventimiglia where he crossed to France, then Spain and eventually to the Portuguese coast. Allegrhia prided herself in their store: The perfect shop window that spoke abundance, panache and catered to the upscale tourist. The shop even exuded a second look from locals despite the daily ordinariness that a routine may bring to daily passersby. She had Iver to thank for that which was matched with her flair for displaying the goods to show their best. Besides, Allegria wouldn't want to leave her aunt Ariana for too long. Since they returned from the war to find each other, they were inseparable: The elderly aunt and her favorite niece.

Ariana turns her back and pushes the mop towards the large open door of the shop, inhaling the breeze that brought about a childhood memory of seashells and her father's fishing net flowing carelessly in the surf. The Murano glass wind chimes, an assortment of them, a chiaroscuro of colors, tinkled and swayed to the breeze. Allegrhia turns as if on cue to offer her tired face to the early afternoon sun. Allegrhia leans the mop against the outer door and takes in the view, the unmistakable scent of the surf assailing her nostrils. She inhales the purity of a

362

tired ocean as the scent of gas exhaust dissipates with the exit of the bus from view, seeking a parking lot. Thick hair flowing to her shoulders, she finally pinned her hair up in a bun and observed the new group of tourists disperse in quest of goods and souvenirs.

Allegria observes the woman and her husband decide to approach her shop. Her practiced eyes told her the two were eager, curious and ready to spend more than she can offer. Two other couples; an elderly woman and her husband in a safari hat, a gay couple, then a small group of older women, heavier and more coiffed, followed behind. The red poppies dress flowed daintily around the young woman's legs, the sandals containing a delicate set of feet matching her delicate twinkling eyes. Allegrhia notices she is pretty in a demure but haughty sort of way. The man appeared almost too confident and followed protectively behind. The young woman looked Italian in a classic sort of way.

Allegrhia turned behind her.

"Iver, don't close for lunch. A new bus just arrived." Allegrhia glanced at her watch and noted the time. Then, the shop was full.

363

# Chapter 2

Lily inhales the scents of the shop. It was like a feast for the senses and eye candy, literally. Unlike Naples, there was a lull in pace, a pronouncedly slower one, with a hint of grace and elegance. She felt her step getting lighter, less fleeting, even brighter. Her pulse slowed as she took in the sounds of the chimes replying to a gentler breeze. The voices here were more acute, the birds resonant, the sunlight unrestricted by buildings and the endless cacophony of vehicle traffic.

There were tables laden with candied pears, apple slices, sliced candied plums, cherries, grapes and even candied pomegranates and persimmons. One table had candied lemon, orange and blood orange rinds in fancy little jars. There was a table that had them to buy by the gram. Then, the chocolates. Papaya slices enrobed in dark chocolate were displayed next to a box tower of Baci chocolates. Tastefully presented, Lily beamed at the prospect of buying a little of each and then a few boxes of Perugina mixed chocolates and truffles. She was in heaven.

Lily muses as her husband Jules roams the tables, tasting here and there the samples proffered on small porcelain dishes. A woman, her dark hair in a thick bun, approached him and offered a slice of persimmon. The same woman who appeared to lazily sweep the shop front and had evaded her eyes. To Lily, she appeared frumpy in her house dress, almost underdressed in comparison to the upscale and sophisticated store. Despite the outfit, Lily sensed she was someone of importance in the shop as she observed the woman re-tie her hair up with a flourish.

365

Lily walked past the gay couple who were merrily sampling lemon rinds and found the woman following behind. "May I try, please?" She queried.

The woman with dark hair in a bun smiled warmly and opened with flair a small jar, taking a small silver tong. She reached in with the silverware and offered it to Lily. Lily reaches with her fingertips and places the candied rind in her mouth, savoring the delicate sweetness.

"I have blood orange and mandarin as well." The woman adds in fluent English.

"How nice," Lily replied. "How should I call you if I need anything?" "Allegria. Please do wander about."

They moved from shelf to shelf, Jules by her elbow, Allegrhia following behind. Iver offers a basket and Lily reaches. Jules winked at Iver, knowing his wife loved to shop.

Lily appeared enthralled. She paused to take in a wall of porcelain which was meant to hold the candied fruit and chocolates. "Oh, gosh. I need to get one of these."

Allegrhia showed her a small jar with blue and yellow daisies daintily painted around the rim and on the lid. "Do you like this one?" Lily's eyes pop, her face breaking into a radiant smile. "I do. How exquisite."

Allegrhia returns a warm smile, handing the young woman the jar, making sure one hand was on the porcelain lid. "Be extra careful as the lid may fall." She counsels.

"I will place this on a shelf in my French kitchen." Lily replied, but her eyes turned down. "Oh, I meant my Italian kitchen." She grinned, appearing embarrassed.

"No problem, miss." Allegrhia adds. "I place this on the counter while you shop, unless you are ready to buy?"

366

"Excusi mio!" Yells one of the older men behind them. A rotund man in a safari hat approaches. Allegrhia turns in time to see the man with a face red from exertion beneath the safari hat. "Mi esposo. Emergencia!"

Alllegrhia eyes Iver, who dashes to an older woman's side, her silver hair cut short in a style. She was slumped on a chair. Another woman, also elderly is busily fanning the woman with a brochure.

"Someone get her a drink." The rotund man in the safari hat comments. "I have it here on the back shelf." Iver offers with efficiency as he dashes with a plastic bottle of water to the elderly woman's side. She sips, but her eyes travel to the ceiling above the shop. She appeared alarmed.

"Look." The woman points to the ceiling.
Something dark swoops over the tourists and exits the shop. The elderly woman screams.
"What is it, madame?" Iver queries as the tourists pause from their ramblings, now riveted to the woman on the chair whose short dress had ridden up to reveal her knees.
"A bat. I think it's a bat." She replies in surprise. Murmurs follow.

Lily touches her hat with both hands, self-consciously pulling down her wide-brimmed hat. "You see anything, Jules? A crow?"
"No, but what is that past the door?" Jules comments as he eyes the deep recesses of the shop in the back. Jules approaches, his curiosity piqued. He makes his way towards the recessed door and walks past the elderly woman sitting slumped as her husband and a few tourists minister over her. More water bottles appear as she continues her story and the dress is pulled down to cover her knees.

367

Past the colorful sunglasses and shelves of postcards, an arched wooden door lay open to a dark corridor beyond. Framed by the wooden door and the darkness were peering eyes, staring out and suspended from the ceiling. The eyes, yellow it seemed, without pupils, look back at Jules in the dark. He pauses and then slowly steps back as his mind attempts to register what he thinks he sees. Allegrhia follows Jules' eyes and quickly rushes towards the door, closing it.

"This way, Mister..." Allegrhia quickly ushers Jules away from the door as she grabs an arm.
"Definitely a bat. You have bats in Salerno?" Jules queries.
Lily turns, holding another container of fruit in a porcelain dish. "I'll get this too dear. For Dorothy's bridal shower."
"Of course. Then we go." Jules punctuates, alarmed over what he thought he saw.
"It's gone. No need to rush." Allegrhia proclaims. Iver approaches. "It's gone. It's a bird. Just a bird." "Oh, dear. There's more here..." Lily saunters to more goods and stretches to reach for chocolates. "Please. Take your time." Allegrhia smiles as she glances at Iver. He winks.

## Chapter 3

It was still light by the time Iver trods towards the square to purchase some eggplants from the corner cart. He normally purchased all the vegetables while Allegria or "Gia", as he and their friends called her, prepared for the day in the early morning as he had had his coffee outside the tobacconist and perused the Neapolitan Times. Today was an exception as he noted the bills that had accumulated from the change drawer on the way out of their shop. While tourists from the bus continued to descend on their shop, encouraged, it seemed, by the woman Lily and the husband in shorts, Iver noted the time and grabbed the cash to make his purchases in time for dinner. The rush to prepare the shop and restock made for a morning without his standard cup of espresso.

Allegrhia, absorbed with her new acquaintance, the woman Lily, who frittered from one sale to another, kept her busy. His wife would be fine, he decided, as she would not be busy for long since the shop closed in an hour. Iver left the shop on foot, hoping the episode with the bat would not recur. It came like a sudden dark cloud on a cheerful day, portentous and foreboding. He found himself tossing the event in his head, his brows furrowing here and there with worry as he passed familiar faces of other local shopkeepers en route.

369

Iver doled out the change as the seller handed him a plastic bag of eggplants. His stomach almost gurgled as he thought of the parmigiana that Gia would make with the help of Ariana. Ariana who still made sheep and goat cheese at home, her deft hands reaching to mix and sieve the milk despite her waning eyesight. Ariana would be napping by now, her afternoon cheese-making done and her clothes mended with care, the stitches familiar by touch.

Today was different, it seemed. The rhythm of the day seemed to ebb and flow without character until tourist season arrived. Then it would feel almost like a rush was upon them to keep placing goods on the storefront, on the shelves and to chase after the teenagers who sometimes loitered around the groups. The teens, avid to obtain the electronics they saw on store shelves and in movies, hoped to get lucky with a forgotten purse or a pocket large enough for their quick hands. Iver hated that. The flow of the day, made more hectic with the push of newcomers,

diesel fumes from buses and locals curious for the unusually-dressed and rusty in speech, made him stumble and stammer. Iver didn't care for the harriedness of it, but it was a welcome as far as his cash and credit store for at least nine months out of the year.

The press of strangers on buses also made for interesting conversation, like the conversation Gia must be having by now with the current haggle of tourists. It made for stories shared and savored in the dead of winter, like

370

the stories he and Gia had about the town and their very own home. Their very own home, which lay empty during the world war, a haven that reappeared unscathed since they were living in a neutral country courtesy of Mussolini. Untouched by war, it seemed, until the day Ariana found her way back with her mother in tow.

Once winter descended upon the town and all the tourist hotspots around Naples, Iver dreaded the nights. Particularly his trips to the cellar. The soot from the logs, the cleaning of the chimney and the sudden drop in temperature when he entered that constant dimness alone. And it wasn't the temperature. It was the way the place made him feel that kept him away in the evening - and to the solace of Gia's arms at night on the highest floor of their stone and terracotta house. Iver could sometimes hear Ariana's snores at night, right across from their bedroom where they agreed she would stay after she left the ground floor bedroom.

Were it not for the cellar at night, Ariana would have been happy to take over the bedroom close to the kitchen, closer to the large hearth. It was larger, had a French door leading to the small courtyard with wisteria and a cat that watched over the goings-on with the adjacent neighbors. However, that was not to be. The cat, a calico, disappeared one day. Gia searched fruitlessly for Olio, a constant companion for Ariana in her twilight years that remained faithful by her side and purred thanks. One late spring Gia found the cat beheaded in the courtyard, its body stiff as an ironing board, its head staring out to space. Iver had grabbed a coal sack and unceremoniously tossed the remains of Olio into it. They felt it was best not to let Ariana know, tender as her heart was at her age of eighty nine.

That same night, the cellar filled with the sound of something growling. The cat, a protective presence, was now gone. In its place was an impenetrable quiet that issued from the cellar and engulfed Iver with loneliness. By the end of the week, Ariana wordlessly sought refuge in the second floor bedroom, dragging her tired legs up and down the stairs to move her bedding and belongings to the second floor bedroom. Iver knew it wasn't his imagination. She too felt the loneliness - the sudden onset of inexplicable sadness that seemed to prevail over the cellar. He pulled her mattress from the room, then the dresser, rolling them up step by step on his homemade trolley. Ariana had welcomed his unspoken permission, then settled in with the sounds of cicadas by her open window. He turned to look and saw Gia by the door, watching.

She knew.

Iver checks the time on his old-fashioned wind-up wristwatch as he edges down the street towards home. The gaggle of children were long gone, now in the haven of their parents' kitchens, watching the food being prepared. It was getting close to seven thirty and the shop would be closed soon. They opened in the old ways: Nine to twelve, closed from twelve to three and reopening from three to eight pm. Sometimes Gia closed early when the last visitor left and walked to their bus or Uber, which the independent and young seem to prefer. As he approached his street, he noted a familiar couple from the tour bus just earlier chatting with none other than Gia by their front door.

CONTINUED

Coming in 2025. On Amazon kindle and paperback. Available where books are sold.

## **About The Author**

Anna Maria Manalo is a recent recipient of the Denis Diderot grant in writing from the international artist residency at Chateau d'Orquevaux in France. Previously a screenwriter, she has placed in the top ten and as a quarterfinalist in several prestigious competitions for her screenplays "The Tulpa Effect", "Under Tango Road" and "Uncharted Darkness." A Master's level therapist and school counselor by profession, she has no training in writing except for three weeks online and a seminar with Robert McKee where she learned the craft of screenwriting.

Since Anna's early retirement in 2020, Anna has authored two titles per year in the genre of paranormal suspense. This book is her seventh published work. She is the first Filipina-American writing in the genre of supernatural suspense nonfiction and fiction.

An avid gardener and patron of the performing arts, Anna has travelled all over the world in quest of unique stories, inspiration and places where her dogs can roam while she writes. When home, she hikes with her husband and two dogs, Quentin Dean and Matisse, cooks international dishes and loves watching sci fi, horror and foreign films.

375

Made in the USA
Columbia, SC
22 July 2024

262e1e6b-9f24-4c86-9a98-3674ab977d0dR01